D0800510

Practice Tests for

IELTS

2

Collins

HarperCollins Publishers
1 London Bridge Street
London
SE1 9GF

First edition 2015

10 9 8 7 6 5 4 3 2 1

© HarperCollins Publishers 2015

ISBN 978-0-00-759813-7

Collins® is a registered trademark of HarperCollins
Publishers Limited

www.collinselt.com

A catalogue record for this book is available from the
British Library

Typeset in India by Aptara

Printed in China by South China Printing Co. Ltd

Written by: Peter Travis
                     Louis Harrison
                     Chia Suan Chong
Illustrations by: Aptara
Audio recordings by: Dsound

Photo credits
P119: **Herbert Kratky**/Shutterstock

Sample answer sheets reproduced with permission of Cambridge English Language
Assessment ©UCLES 2015.

If any copyright holders have been omitted, please contact the Publisher who will make
the necessary arrangements at the first opportunity.

Contents

Title	Topic	Page number
Introduction		4
Overview of the IELTS examination		6
Strategies for success		8
Test 1	Listening	31
	Reading	39
	Writing	50
	Speaking	52
Test 2	Listening	53
	Reading	61
	Writing	71
	Speaking	73
Test 3	Listening	74
	Reading	82
	Writing	93
	Speaking	95
Test 4	Listening	96
	Reading	101
	Writing	112
	Speaking	114
General Training Test A	Reading	115
	Writing	125
General Training Test B	Reading	126
	Writing	139
Mini-dictionary		140
Audio script		156
Sample answer sheets		172
Listening and Reading answer key		175
Writing: model answers		178
Speaking: model answers		183
Acknowledgements		190

Introduction

Who is this book for?

Practice Tests for IELTS 2 will prepare you for the IELTS test whether you are taking the test for the first time or re-sitting it. It has been written for learners with band score 5–5.5 who are trying to achieve band score 6 or higher. The book, with its answer key and model answers, has been designed so that you can use the materials to study on your own. However, the book can also be used as part of IELTS preparation classes.

Content

Practice Tests for IELTS 2 is divided into three sections. The first section contains an introduction, an overview of the IELTS test, and strategies for success in the test. The second section contains four complete Academic tests and two General Training tests for Reading and Writing. The third section contains a mini-directory, a full audio script, sample answer sheets, answer keys for the Listening and Reading components, and model answers for the Writing and Speaking questions.

Specifically, the book contains:

- **Tips for success** – essential advice for success in the test
- an **Overview of the IELTS test** – a quick reference to IELTS whenever you need to remind yourself of what to expect on exam day
- **Strategies for success** – advice about how to tackle each of the components in the test
- **Common errors** – some common errors that candidates might make when taking the IELTS test and how to avoid these common errors
- **Practice tests** – four complete Academic tests and two General Training tests for Reading and Writing
- **Mini-dictionary** – definitions and examples of the most important high-level vocabulary from *Practice Tests for IELTS 2* (definitions are from Collins COBUILD dictionaries)
- **Audio script** – the full texts of what you will hear in the Listening and Speaking components
- **Sample answer sheets** – familiarise yourself with the answer sheets used in the Listening, Reading and Writing components of the IELTS test
- **Answer keys** – the answers for all the questions in the Listening and Reading components
- **Model answers** – example answers for the Writing and Speaking components, all of which would achieve the highest marks in the IELTS test
- **CD** – MP3 files with all of the Listening passages, questions from the Speaking components and the model answers for the Speaking components.

Other IELTS resources

This is the second book of practice tests. If you would like more practice tests, there are four more practice tests in *Collins Practice Tests for IELTS* (ISBN 978-0-00-749969-4).

Collins also offer a wide range of exam preparation books, including our Skills for IELTS series (*Reading for IELTS, Writing for IELTS, Listening for IELTS,* and *Speaking for IELTS*) and our *IELTS Dictionary*. Please go to www.collinselt.com to find these and other resources.

Tips for success

Make a plan to succeed and start by following these tips.

- **Register for the test early.** If you are applying for university, check the application deadlines. Make sure that you register to take the test well before the deadline to ensure that your scores arrive on time.
- **Find out the score requirements for the universities you want to apply for.** Degree programmes that have minimum-score requirements typically post them on their admissions websites.
- **Start to study early.** The more you practise, the more you will improve your skills. Give yourself at least one month to complete all of the practice tests in this book. Spend at least one hour a day studying and don't give up. Remember, by using this book, you are on your way to high scores in the IELTS test!
- **Time yourself** when you complete the practice tests.
- Don't be afraid to make your own notes on the book. For example, writing down the definitions to words you don't know will help you remember them later on.
- Read or listen to the model answers as many times as you need to.
- In the Writing component, return to the questions and try to come up with new responses. Keep practising until creating responses within the time limits becomes easy for you.

Using the book for self-study

Having access to someone who can provide informed feedback on your answers to the Writing and Speaking questions is an advantage. However, you can still learn a lot working on your own or with a study partner who is willing to give and receive feedback.

Ideally, you should begin by working through the *Strategies for success* for each part of the test. Reading this section will help you know what mistakes to avoid when doing the practice tests.

When you are ready to try the practice tests, make sure you attempt the Writing and Speaking tasks. These are skills that can only be improved through extensive practice. At the same time, you should aim to become well informed about a wide variety of subjects, not just those covered in the book. The IELTS Writing and Speaking components can cover almost any topic considered to be within the grasp of a well-educated person.

Practise writing to a time limit. If you find this difficult at first, you could focus first on writing a high-quality response of the correct length. Then you could start to reduce the time allowed gradually until you are able to write an acceptable answer within the time limit. You should become familiar enough with your own handwriting to be able to accurately estimate the number of words you have written at a glance.

Model answers should be studied to identify the underlying approach and effect on the reader. Do not memorise essays or letters or attempt to fit a pre-existing response around another test question. By working through the practice tests in the book, you should develop the skills and language to effectively express your own responses to unseen test questions on the day.

Overview of the IELTS examination

The International English Language Testing System (IELTS) is jointly managed by the British Council, Cambridge ESOL Examinations and IDP Education, Australia.

There are two versions of the test:
- Academic
- General Training.

The Academic test is for students wishing to study at undergraduate or postgraduate level in an English-medium environment.

The General Training test is for people who wish to migrate to an English-speaking country.

There are separate Reading and Writing components for the Academic and General Training IELTS tests.

The test
There are four components to the test.

Listening	30 minutes, plus 10 minutes for transferring answers to the answer sheet. There are 4 sections in this part of the test.
Reading	60 minutes. There are 3 texts in this component, with 40 questions to answer.
Writing	60 minutes. There are 2 writing tasks. Your answer for Task 1 should have a minimum of 150 words. Your answer for Task 2 should have a minimum of 250 words.
Speaking	11–14 minutes. There are 3 parts in this component. This part of the test will be recorded.

Timetabling – Listening, Reading and Writing must be taken on the same day, and in the order listed above. Speaking can be taken up to seven days before or after the other components.

Scoring – Each component of the test is given a band score. The average of the four scores produces the Overall Band Score. You do not pass or fail IELTS; you receive a score.

IELTS and the Common European Framework of Reference
The CEFR shows the level of the learner and is used for many English as a Foreign Language examinations. The table below shows the approximate CEFR level and the equivalent IELTS Overall Band Score.

CEFR description	CEFR code	IELTS Band Score
Proficient user	C2	9
(Advanced)	C1	7–8
Independent user	B2	5–6.5
(Intermediate – Upper Intermediate)	B1	4–5

This table contains the general descriptors for the band scores 1–9.

IELTS Band Scores		
9	Expert user	Has fully operational command of the language: appropriate, accurate and fluent with complete understanding
8	Very good user	Has fully operational command of the language, with only occasional unsystematic inaccuracies and inappropriacies. Misunderstandings may occur in unfamiliar situations. Handles complex detailed argumentation well
7	Good user	Has operational command of the language, though with occasional inaccuracies, inappropriacies and misunderstandings in some situations. Generally handles complex language well and understands detailed reasoning
6	Competent user	Has generally effective command of the language despite some inaccuracies, inappropriacies and misunderstandings. Can use and understand fairly complex language, particularly in familiar situations
5	Modest user	Has partial command of the language, coping with overall meaning in most situations, though is likely to make many mistakes. Should be able to handle basic communication in own field
4	Limited user	Basic competence is limited to familiar situations. Has frequent problems in understanding and expression. Is not able to use complex language
3	Extremely limited user	Conveys and understands only general meaning in very familiar situations. Frequent breakdowns in communication occur
2	Intermittent user	No real communication is possible except for the most basic information using isolated words or short formulae in familiar situations and to meet immediate needs. Has great difficulty understanding spoken and written English
1	Non user	Essentially has no ability to use the language beyond possibly a few isolated words
0	Did not attempt the test	No assessable information provided

Marking

The Listening and Reading components have 40 items, each worth one mark if correctly answered. Here are some examples of how marks are translated into band scores.

Listening   16 out of 40 correct answers: band score 5
                   23 out of 40 correct answers: band score 6
                   30 out of 40 correct answers: band score 7

Reading   15 out of 40 correct answers: band score 5
                   23 out of 40 correct answers: band score 6
                   30 out of 40 correct answers: band score 7

Writing and Speaking are marked according to performance descriptors.

Writing – Examiners award a band score for each of four areas with equal weighting:
- Task achievement (Task 1)
- Task response (Task 2)
- Coherence and cohesion
- Lexical resource and grammatical range and accuracy

Speaking – Examiners award a band score for each of four areas with equal weighting:
- Fluency and coherence
- Lexical resource
- Grammatical range
- Accuracy and pronunciation

For full details of how the examination is scored and marked, go to: **www.ielts.org**.

Strategies for success

Listening

The IELTS Listening component consists of four sections, each containing 10 questions.

Section 1: The recording is of a conversation between two speakers in an everyday social situation.

Section 2: The recording is of a monologue in an everyday social situation.

Section 3: The recording is of a conversation between two to four people in an educational or training situation.

Section 4: The recording is of a monologue on an academic subject.

The test takes approximately 30 minutes and consists of 40 questions, each worth one mark. The recording is played once only. You will then have 10 minutes at the end of the test to transfer your answers to an answer sheet.

Here are some tips for preparing yourself for the Listening component.

- **Get used to listening to a range of accents**

  You might hear a variety of accents, including British, American and Australian in the recording. You might have difficulty understanding if you are not familiar with an accent, so practise as much as possible by watching films and video clips that feature accents that you are less used to hearing. Listening to English language radio online might help too.

- **Familiarise yourself with different task types**

  While you might be familiar with task types like multiple choice or short answers, you might need practice in other task types, e.g. table/flow-chart completion, matching, labelling a diagram, chart or map. Complex diagrams or graphs may look intimidating but the questions are often easy once you understand what to listen out for.

- **Try to answer all the questions**

  There is no penalty for wrong answers, so if in doubt, guess the answer to a question. You might be right.

- **Follow the order of information in the recording (unless the task requires re-ordering)**

  The questions follow the order of the information in the recording. This means that the answer for question 2 will probably come later in the recording than the answer for question 1, so do not feel you have to focus on all the questions at the same time when you are listening.

- **Pay attention if you hear someone spelling a word**

  You might hear someone in a recording confirming the spelling of a word, often a name, e.g. *The surname is Goforth, G–O–F–O–R–T–H.* If a word or name is spelt out, it is very likely that it is the answer to one of the questions. Make sure you know how to say the letters of the alphabet in English, especially the vowels.

- **Practise listening to numbers**

  You might be required to write down telephone numbers or other large numbers (e.g. 852,091). Practise by asking a friend or family member to read out a variety of large numbers while you write them down. Alternatively, listen to the news or radio programmes in English and write down any numbers you hear.

Common errors

Trying to read the questions, listen to the recording and write the answers all at the same time can put the multi-tasking skills of a candidate to the test. As the recording is played once only, this can add to the stress. Here are some common errors that candidates make when doing the Listening component and how to avoid them.

1 Not paying attention to the example in the recording

At the start of the Listening component, you might hear a variation of the following instructions.

> **Example (Listening Section 1)**
> *Now turn to Section 1. You will hear a conversation between a travel agent and a student. First, you have time to look at questions 1–8.*
>
> *You will see that there is an example that has been done for you. ... So the answer 'Morzine' has already been written in the gap.*

Some candidates choose not to listen to the example question, seeing it as a waste of time. However, the example not only provides a model for that particular question type, it also helps set the context. A good grasp of the context can provide a framework for you to understand the information that you will hear.

When listening to the example, ask yourself the following questions.
- Who are the speakers in this conversation?
- Where are they?
- What do they want from each other?
- What information will they need from each other?

This will prepare you for the rest of the conversation.

2 Spending the time between sections worrying about answers in the last section

Use the time before the beginning of a new section to read the instructions and questions. Underline the key words so that you can listen for the important information in the recording. Try to predict what the answers might be. If the task is a gap-fill, ask yourself: *What kind of word could complete that gap? What part of speech? A verb, a noun, an adjective, an adverb? If a verb, what form of verb? If a noun, singular or plural? If an adjective, positive or negative meaning?* Even if your predictions are wrong, the act of predicting will help you to listen out for the correct answer.

Remember: You hear each recording once only, so understanding what you are being asked and what to look out for is crucial.

At the end of the Listening component, you have 10 minutes to transfer your answers to the answer sheet, so write your answers on the question paper while you are listening. There is plenty of time at the end to check your spelling and copy your answers carefully onto the answer sheet. When transferring your answers, make sure you write your answers next to the correct question number. Also, check that your answers comply with the instructions. For example, if the instructions were *Write NO MORE THAN TWO WORDS or A NUMBER for each answer,* do not write three words.

> **Tip: Manage your time wisely**
> Do this by:
> - using the time before listening to the recording for each section to read the questions and predict the answers
> - using the 10 minutes at the end of the Listening component to transfer your answers carefully to the answer sheet, checking for mistakes.

3   Jumping to conclusions and getting the wrong answer

When listening out for answers to a question, some candidates immediately assume they have the answer when some of the words in the recording match the words in a question.

> **Example (Listening, all sections)**
> *Which of the following are provided by student accommodation services?*
> *A   breakfast, lunch and dinner*
> *B   advice about weekend jobs*
> *C   use of a washing machine, dishwasher and computer printer*
> *D   an en-suite toilet and shower room*

Now here is an extract from the recording.

> *Aside from providing you with a roof over your head and a bed to sleep on, student accommodation services also offer the use of a communal washing machine, dishwasher and refrigerator for your convenience. Students are offered full board and all rooms have an en-suite toilet and bath ... Oh, sorry! I meant en-suite toilet and shower. We are also happy to give you advice about what you can do in the city over the weekends.*

Can you guess why some candidates might wrongly choose option B or C? The audio script says *advice about what you can do in the city*, which is not the same as *advice about weekend jobs*, and the use of a refrigerator is not the same as the use of a computer printer. Yet many candidates are too quick to move on to the next question. Phrases like *Oh, sorry! I mean ...* are common and signal that an important correction to what has been said is about to follow.

Tip: Listen out for traps
Do this by:
• listening carefully to the end of an utterance
• not making assumptions based on one or two words you hear that match a question
• listening for phrases or words that negate what was said previously.

4   Staying up all night before the test to revise

As you listen, you will have to read (and re-read) the questions, figure out the correct answers and write them down. That is a lot to do in a short time, so the Listening component requires a lot of concentration. You need to be alert, so make sure you get lots of rest beforehand.

To prepare for the Listening component, practise reading, listening and writing at the same time. Here are some ways to do this.
• Print out the script from the scene of a film. Watch the scene while reading the script and circling key words.
• Listen to the evening news in English while at the same time looking at that day's English newspaper, and try to find the same news story or facts in the newspaper.
• Write a summary of a film dialogue or news story as you watch or listen to it.
• Ask a friend to tell you a number of things in English, e.g. the foods they like, reasons why they love living in a city, the features of their new smartphone. Write them down as your friend is speaking.

5   Not analysing why an answer was incorrect

Some candidates do the listening sections of practice tests but then they just check their answers in the answer key and add up their marks; they fail to ask themselves why they got an incorrect answer. Refer to the audio script or listen to the recording again to see where you have gone wrong and learn from your mistakes.

Checklist:

✓ Use the example to help you understand the context.
✓ Read the questions before the recording starts and predict the answers.
✓ In the last 10 minutes, transfer your answers carefully to the answer sheet.
✓ Listen carefully and make sure the answer matches what was said.
✓ Get enough sleep before the test to ensure you are alert.
✓ Practise listening, reading and writing at the same time.
✓ When doing practice tests, learn from your mistakes by studying the audio script.

Reading

The IELTS Reading component consists of three reading passages. The texts for the Academic test come from authentic sources such as magazines, journals, books and newspapers, while texts for the General Training test could also include advertisements, leaflets and instruction manuals.

The Reading component takes 60 minutes and there are 40 questions.

Here are some tips for preparing yourself for both the Academic and the General Training Reading component.

• Read widely

As the reading passages are based on authentic materials, reading newspapers, blogposts, magazines, books, etc. will help to familiarise you with different styles of writing (descriptive, discursive, argumentative, etc.) and expose you to a variety of language about different topics. It will also help you to practise dealing with unknown words and topics – a skill that comes in very useful during the test.

• Be prepared for the fact that the reading passages get more difficult

The first reading passage is the easiest of the three, so try not to spend too much time on it. It is also the one for which you could score the most marks, so ensure you check your answers to the questions and avoid careless mistakes.

The third passage is the most difficult of all, but do not get disheartened when you are tackling the questions based on it. Remember that the IELTS test is graded from 0 to 9 and there are bound to be difficult questions designed to distinguish between candidates who will get a band score of 7 or 8 from those who deserve a band score of 9.

• Do not make careless spelling and grammar mistakes

When you are copying words from a passage, make sure you spell them correctly; spelling mistakes will cost you marks.

• Find the topic sentence of each paragraph

The topic sentence summarises the main idea or expresses the main point of a paragraph. It is often the first sentence of a paragraph, but it can be anywhere in a paragraph. Can you find the topic sentence in the following paragraph?

Example (Reading, all parts)
The pressures and deadlines a person faces at work are often blamed for causing stress, but stress can also come from a lack of recognition and appreciation for the work someone does. If someone suffers from a stress-related illness, the first step to getting better is to identify the cause. Stress can also be exacerbated by the lack of support from family members. Understanding its causes can help people to actively seek a solution to the problem.

Identifying the topic sentence of a paragraph (in this case, *Understanding its causes [the causes of stress] can help people to actively seek a solution to the problem*), will give you a better idea about what the paragraph is about, and this will help you to find information in the passage more quickly. Moreover, finding the topic sentence helps greatly in tasks where you are required to match headings to paragraphs.

Common errors

Candidates often panic when they see the extent of the passages they have to read and the number of questions they have to answer. Here are some common errors that candidates make when doing the Reading component, and how to avoid them.

1   Reading the passage before you know what is expected of you

When you read the instructions and the questions, make sure you understand what you are required to do. Circle key words to remind yourself what is important when referring back to the question. Remember:

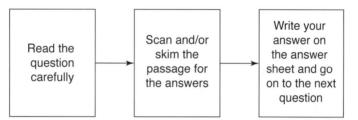

Which key words would you circle in the question below?

Example (Reading, all sections)
Which paragraphs, A–D, contain information about the following?

Write the correct letter, A–D, in boxes 20–23 on your answer sheet. You may use any letter more than once.

A   *the contents of the contract*
B   *how to sue your employer successfully for unfair dismissal*
C   *flexible working hours*
D   *childcare facilities*

You could circle *Write the correct letter* and *boxes 20-23*. This is important as you would lose marks if you wrote:

20   flexible working hours

instead of

20   C

You could also circle *use any letter more than once* because even if you had already used a letter, you could use it again.

Sometimes, the questions or options are long, e.g. *how to sue your employer successfully for unfair dismissal*. Consider circling the key words *sue*, *employer* and *unfair dismissal* so that it is easier to look out for information when you skim and scan the passage.

Tip: Read the question carefully before looking for the answer
Do this by:
• making sure you understand the instructions
• circling the key words in the question.

2 Wasting time by reading every word in a passage

Not every part of a passage has relevant information. Look for linking words and adverbs to guide you, e.g. *What two problems do experts face when they are restoring a work of art?*

When skimming a paragraph on art restoration, consider looking for synonyms for *problems* and find linking words or adverbs that signal that there are two aspects to the answer. When you think you have found them, read the paragraph again more carefully.

> **Useful phrases: Linking two ideas**
> *The pigments used to restore a painting can affect the original material. **Another** difficulty is the irreversible damage that the cleaning process can cause.*
>
> ***First**, the pigments used to restore a painting can affect the original material, and **second**, the cleaning process can cause irreversible damage.*
>
> *The pigments used to restore a painting can affect the original material. **Also**, the cleaning process can cause irreversible damage.*
>
> ***Both** the pigments used to restore a painting **and** the cleaning process can cause irreversible damage, and these are just two of the complications that art restorers must consider.*
>
> ***In addition to** the potentially deleterious effects of the pigments used to restore a painting, the art restorer **also** has to contend with the irreversible damage that can be caused by the cleaning process.*

3 Worrying if you do not understand some of the words

Try to guess the meaning of unknown words from the context. Look for synonyms or other clues to help you. In the example below, what might a *saloon* be?

> **Example (Reading, all sections)**
> *The saloon, also known as the sedan, typically has an engine in the front and a boot in the rear, and can have two or four doors. Unlike station wagons, saloons do not typically have a roof that extends rearward.*

Even if you do not know the synonym *sedan*, you know that a *saloon* has an engine, a boot, two or four doors and a roof, and is different from a *station wagon*. Could you guess that a *saloon* is a kind of car?

> **Tip: Guess the meaning of words you do not know**
> Do this by:
> * looking for synonyms, paraphrases or other clues that may help to explain the word
> * looking for antonyms, e.g. *A **gigantic** man, he looked out of place in that **tiny** room*
> * looking for a category to which a word might belong, e.g. *saloon – vehicle*; *poodle – dog – animal*; *daffodil – flower – plant*.

4 Running out of time

You have 60 minutes to read three passages and answer 40 questions, so do not spend too long on any one question. If you get stuck and you realise that you have spent the last 5 minutes trying to answer a question, make an intelligent guess at what the answer might be and move on.

Write your answers directly on the answer sheet, not the question paper; in the Reading component, unlike the Listening component, you do not have an extra 10 minutes at the end to transfer your answers to the answer sheet.

You must write your answers in pencil, so make sure you have an eraser with you so that you can change your answers if necessary.

> **Tip: Time is very important – do not waste it**
> Do this by:
> • not spending too much time on any one question
> • writing your answers directly on the answer sheet.

5 Feeling disheartened when you do practice tests

Practice is important, but if you keep getting approximately the same score each time you complete a practice paper, it is a good idea to take a break, expand your vocabulary through other kinds of reading activities and find different ways to practise skimming and scanning skills.

Here are some ideas.
• Skim a newspaper looking for a particular story referred to on the front page. How fast can you find it?
• Practise skimming a newspaper article or a webpage as quickly as possible. Can you summarise the text?
• Find out what people are saying about a particular event e.g. the World Cup, a celebrity marriage or a new film on Twitter or Facebook. Skim the comments and summarise what the general sentiment is. Are people positive or negative about the event? Why? What do they think might happen?
• Scan a newspaper article for synonyms or near synonyms of words in the headlines.
• Scan a text for numbers and/or names as quickly as you can.
• The next time you are looking for information on the internet, conduct your search in English and scan quickly for a possible website, ignoring all irrelevant results.

Checklist:

✓ Read questions carefully before you read a passage to find the answers.

✓ Look for linking words and adverbials to help point you towards the correct answers.

✓ Use the context to help you to work out the meaning of unknown words.

✓ If you get stuck on a difficult question, guess the answer and move on to the next question.

✓ Write your answers directly on the answer sheet.

✓ Practise your skimming and scanning skills.

Writing

The IELTS Writing component takes 60 minutes and consists of two tasks. Task 2 carries more weight in marking than Task 1.

Academic Writing component

Task 1 requires you to describe, summarise or explain the information given in a diagram, graph, table or chart. You may be asked to:
- describe and explain data
- describe the stages of a process
- explain how something works
- describe an object or event.

Task 2 requires you to write an essay in response to a point of view, argument or problem.

Both tasks in the Academic Writing component must be in a formal style.

General Training Writing component

In Task 1 you are given a situation and you are required to write a semi-formal or formal letter requesting information or explaining the situation.

Task 2 requires you to write an essay in response to a point of view, argument or problem. The essay can be slightly more personal in style than the Academic Writing Task 2 essay.

In Task 2 of both the Academic Writing component and the General Training Writing component, you may have to write one of the following types of essay:
- agree or disagree – This requires you to give your own opinion.
- for and against – This requires you to discuss both sides of a question, and your own opinion might only become clear in the conclusion.
- problem and solution – This requires you to explain a problem and suggest possible solutions.

Here are some tips for preparing yourself for the individual tasks in the Writing component.

- ## Academic Writing Task 1

  Your essay should have three parts: an introduction, the main body and a conclusion.

  Introduction

  In your introduction, summarise the information in the diagram, graph, table or chart by rephrasing the question. Avoid copying words and phrases from the question.

Examples (Academic Writing Task 1)
Question: *The chart below shows how many people go to work using trains, the underground, and bus services every day.*

Introduction: *The chart illustrates the number of people commuting daily using different modes of public transportation.*

Question 2: *The diagrams show the average male and female retirement ages in five different countries.*

Introduction: *The pie charts illustrate how old the men and women of Japan, UK, Algeria, Kenya and India are when they stop working.*

Main body

The main body should consist of two or three paragraphs, each presenting information illustrated in the diagrams, graphs, tables or charts. Try to highlight and describe at least three key pieces of information. Practise looking at diagrams, graphs, tables and charts and picking out the most relevant or interesting information.

Conclusion

The conclusion should consist of two or three sentences that summarise what you have written. You could rephrase your introduction and highlight key information from the main body of your essay.

• General Training Writing Task 1

Your letter should have three parts: an introductory paragraph, the main body and some concluding remarks.

The introductory paragraph should consist of one to two sentences stating your reason for writing. In the main body, provide the required information, explaining and giving examples to illustrate what you are saying. In your concluding remarks, say what you expect to happen or what you hope will be done, and sign off in a style appropriate to the purpose of the letter.

• Academic and General Training Writing Task 2

> **Example (Academic and General Training Writing Task 2)**
> Question: *Online shopping is gaining popularity these days but some people believe that it is overrated and problematic.*

Introduction

The introduction should consist of about two to four sentences and provide a general framework for the essay. Here are some suggestions.
o Sentence 1: Describe the background to the situation/topic and/or describe the current situation, e.g. *Nowadays, many people prefer to shop online than to go shopping in traditional high street stores.*
o Sentence 2: State the problem, the controversy or the argument, e.g. *However, online shopping has its own set of problems.*
o Sentence 3: Briefly outline both sides of the issue and/or give your own opinion (depending on the question type and what you include in the body of your essay), e.g. *While some people enjoy the convenience of internet shopping, others worry about not getting what they ordered and issues of privacy.*

Main body

The main body should consist of two to three paragraphs, each making a point relevant to the argument/discussion. Here are some suggestions.
o Write a topic sentence that expresses the main point of your paragraph, e.g. *Internet shopping seems better suited to certain products than others.*
o Write one or more sentences to explain and/or provide evidence to support the point in the topic sentence, e.g. *You cannot test drive a car or try on a suit if you purchase one online, but when it comes to plane tickets, books or music, a traditional store cannot provide much added value.*

o End your paragraph with a sentence that summarises the paragraph and ties it to the topic sentence and the question, e.g. *Online shopping is ideal for items that do not need to be seen in real life, tried on or tested, and shoppers are more likely to take advantage of the internet when they purchase these things.*

<u>Conclusion</u>

The conclusion summarises what you discussed and refers the reader back to the main argument in the question. Here, you can state or re-state your point of view, e.g. *As we can see, despite the obvious benefits of online shopping, there are also disadvantages that come with the convenience. However, even though it is not all good, I personally think that the pros far outweigh the cons, and I am convinced that internet shopping will continue to grow in the near future.*

Common errors

The writing tasks are a chance to demonstrate the range and accuracy of your knowledge of English and your ability to organise your writing in coherent and well-structured paragraphs while answering the task question. However, certain kinds of mistake can cause you to lose marks. Here are some common errors that candidates make in the Writing component. Numbers 1–5 refer to the Writing components in both the Academic and General Training tests; 6–8 refer to Academic Writing Task 1; 9–10 refer to General Training Task 1; and 11–13 refer to both the Academic and General Training Task 2.

The Writing component in general

1 Writing less than the minimum word count

For Task 1 the minimum word count is 150 words. For Task 2 it is 250 words. Writing fewer words will affect your score significantly; a short answer also tends to affect coherence and will not allow you to demonstrate the full range and accuracy of your knowledge of English.

Some candidates write too little because they spend too long on one task, and as a result do not have enough time for the other. You have 60 minutes for both parts of the Writing component, and it is recommended that you spend about 20 minutes on Task 1 and 40 minutes on Task 2. Task 2 carries more marks than Task 1, so work out your strategy. Would you choose to do Task 2 first?

2 Not planning your answer

Because of the time pressure, it is tempting to put pen to paper immediately after reading the question. However, if you do not think about the question, plan your essay and draft it, your writing may be badly organised and lack intelligible content.

You will not be marked only on the range of structures and vocabulary you use, but also for task achievement/response, cohesion and coherence. This means that your answer must be relevant to the question and the examiner must be able to follow what you are saying easily.

Spend about 3 minutes thinking about the questions and planning and drafting your answer for Task 1, and 5 minutes doing the same for Task 2. The clearer your response is in your mind, the better you will be able to focus on grammatical structures and vocabulary while you are writing. You will not be given any rough paper in the test, so use the question sheet to plan your essay, but remember to strike through your draft to show the examiner that it is not part of your answer.

3 Repeating the same structures or words

> **Example (Academic Writing Task 1)**
> *Women in Singapore are expected to live until they are 84 years old and men are expected to live until they are 80 years old. However, in Myanmar women are expected to live until they are 67 years old and men are expected to live until they are 63 years old. The longest life expectancy is in Japan, where women are expected to live until they are 86 years old and men are expected to live until they are 79 years old.*

Did you notice that the facts about the three countries were described using the same sentence structure? How does the example below vary sentence structures?

> **Example (Academic Writing Task 1)**
> *While women in Singapore have a life expectancy of 84 years, men are expected to live until they are 80. However, in Myanmar, life expectancy is significantly shorter, with the average female living until she is 67 years of age and the average male until he is 63. Conversely, Japanese women tend to live to the age of 86, and the life expectancy of Japanese men is about 79 years.*

> **Tip: Vary sentence structures and vocabulary**
> Do this by:
> • making a verb or verb phrase into a noun, e.g. *expected to live* —→ *life expectancy*
> • using synonyms or paraphrasing, e.g. *the average woman/man* —→ *the average female/ male*; *67 years of age* —→ *the age of 67* —→ *67 years old*
> • beginning sentences with different noun phrases, e.g. *While women in Singapore* —→ *in Myanmar, life expectancy* ... .

4 Memorising model answers

Reproducing memorised answers constitutes plagiarism; this is a serious offence. The IELTS examination board have strategies in place to spot memorised answers and offenders will be severely penalised. In addition, questions in the actual test are likely to be different from questions in practice tests, so if a candidate tries to reproduce a memorised answer, it will not answer the question. Furthermore, if a candidate tries to adapt a memorised answer to a test question, his/her writing will probably become difficult to follow. This in turn affects the score for cohesion and coherence. Finally, a memorised answer would also mask your real abilities, and the examiner would not be able to judge your knowledge of English adequately.

5 Translating an answer from your first language

The writing convention in every language is unique, so the structure and style you would use and the way you would write an answer to a question in your own language (whether an essay, a letter or a description of a graph) would vary from what is required in English. In English, we tend to write a topic sentence before elaborating on it, but this might be less common in other languages and cultures.

Drafting an answer in your own language and then translating it into English is not only time-consuming, but can result in an incoherent piece of writing. Furthermore, you could end up not using appropriate collocations, idioms and set phrases; these are often lost in translation.

Start thinking about your answer in English from the planning stage and you will be more likely to remember interesting words and phrases.

Checklist:
✓ Write at least 150 words for Task 1 and 250 words for Task 2.

✓ Spend some time thinking about and planning your answer.

✓ Find different ways to express similar ideas and vary your sentence structure.

✓ Avoid memorising model answers.

✓ Think about your answer in English from the planning stage.

Academic Writing Task 1

6   Describing every single detail

There is sometimes more information than you need in the diagrams, graphs, tables or charts provided. If you tried to describe every detail, you would risk sacrificing the cohesion and coherence of your writing. The main features of the diagram might be lost, which would make it difficult for the reader to focus on what is important.

In the example below, the candidate tried to describe three line graphs showing the sales of CDs, cassettes and music downloads. The extract is from his description of CD sales. Notice how difficult it is to pick out the important information.

> **Example (Academic Writing Task 1)**
> *The sale of CDs in the United States started rising in the mid-eighties, and in 1990 it hit 250 million a year and then increased further to 620 million in the mid-nineties. Growth slowed down slightly and after peaking at 790 million in 1996, it fell to 780 million in 1997, and then increased again to reach another peak in 1999 at 980 million. Sales then plateaued for a year before dropping to 880 million in 2000. They rose to 900 million in 2001 but dipped sharply to 780 million in 2002. They then went up a little in 2003 and then fell again to 700 million in 2004.*

It is far better to choose the most significant information from each category and highlight it. If you spend too much time describing information about one category, you will not have time to compare and contrast the information with the other categories. In the example below, the candidate highlighted the key features of CD sales. He then compared and contrasted these features with the other categories.

> **Example (Academic Writing Task 1)**
> *The sale of CDs in the United States started rising in the mid-eighties to hit a peak in 1999 at 980 million a year as cassette sales fell to 180 million in the same year. After plateauing for a year, there was a downward trend for CDs, with sales dropping to 700 million in 2004. This coincided with the rise of music downloads, which started tentatively in 1997, but rocketed ...*

> Tip: Highlight the most important information in diagrams, graphs, tables or charts
> Do this by:
> • identifying key features of the diagrams, graphs, tables or charts
> • comparing and contrasting information across categories.

7 Not giving actual figures or units of measurement

What is missing from the following examples?

Example (Academic Writing Task 1)
A
The largest number of mobile phones can be seen in China, with India trailing close behind. Although the USA comes third in the list, there are only a third as many mobile phones as in China.

B
In 1950, 1000 were used for agricultural purposes, while only 100 were used for industrial purposes. In 2000, the amount of water used for agricultural purposes increased to 3000.

In A the candidate described mobile phone ownership in several countries, but failed to give concrete figures to support what she was saying. She could potentially have avoided losing marks for task achievement by providing actual figures, e.g. *The highest number of mobile phones can be seen in China at 990 million, with India trailing close behind at 880 million. Although the USA comes third in the list at 310 million mobile phones, there are only a third as many mobile phones as in China.*

In B, the candidate gave figures but no units of measurement, so we do not know what the figures refer to. Always include units of measurement so that the information is clear, e.g. *In 1950, 1000 km^3 of water were used for agricultural purposes, while only 100 km^3 were used for industrial purposes. In 2000, the amount of water used for agricultural purposes increased to 3000 km^3.*

8 Misinterpreting the question or the diagrams, graphs, tables or charts

In the example below, the candidate attempted to provide figures and units of measurement, but what do you think went wrong?

Example (Academic Writing Task 1)
In 1927, only one American was unemployed, but this rose to 12 in 1933.

Clearly, more than one American must have been unemployed in 1927. The candidate had failed to see that the Y-axis specified 'Unemployment (in millions)'. The correct description of the graph would read: *In 1927, only one million Americans were unemployed, but this rose to 12 million in 1933.*

If you are not used to looking at diagrams and graphs, you could find them difficult and intimidating. Practise interpreting diagrams and graphs and familiarise yourself with them. There are plenty of good examples online.

In an attempt to paraphrase the question, some candidates make inaccurate generalisations, e.g. *The pie chart shows different literacy rates in the world*, when in fact, the pie chart shows literacy rates in five different countries. Make sure you do not report facts inaccurately; this could lead to a loss of marks in task achievement.

Checklist:
✓ Pick out the key information in the diagrams, graphs, tables or charts.

✓ Support your description with actual figures.

✓ Remember to include units of measurement.

✓ Check that you have not misread the question or the diagrams, graphs, tables or charts.

General Writing Task 1
9   Using the wrong register

Writing in an informal style to someone to whom you should be writing in a formal style, and vice versa, demonstrates a lack of knowledge of the conventions of letter writing. Before you start writing, ask yourself: *Who am I writing to? What is the purpose of the letter?*

Learn phrases that differentiate a formal letter from an informal one. Which phrases in the example below are formal and which are informal? Which would you use when writing to the manager of a hotel? Which would you use when writing to a friend?

Useful phrases: Beginning and ending a letter	
Dear Sir/Madam / Dear Mr/Ms/Mrs Webster *I'm writing with regard to ... / I'm writing to inform you that ...*	*Dear Jen* *How are you? It's been a long time since I last saw you. I hope you are well.*

Useful phrases: Beginning and ending a letter	
Should you need any further information, please feel free to contact me at ... *I look forward to seeing/hearing from you soon.* *Yours faithfully,* *Sienna Ford*	*Anyway, thanks/sorry again for ...* *Hope to see you soon. / I can't wait to see you soon!* *Love* *Sienna*

Tip: Write your letter in the appropriate style/register
Do this by:
• knowing who you are writing to
• learning the difference between formal and informal expressions
• learning fixed expressions for beginning and ending letters.

10 Not addressing all the points in a question

Below is an example of a Task 1 question. Note: There are usually three points that the candidate has to address.

Example (General Writing Task 1)
You are staying in rented accommodation arranged for you by the school you are studying at. However, you feel that the landlord has not provided the facilities that the school promised you.

Write a letter of complaint to the school's accommodation services and ask for a change in your accommodation. In your letter
- *say what the school had promised you*
- *describe the current unsatisfactory situation*
- *ask for changes to be made.*

The three points given are not just guidelines but essential to task achievement. Failure to address each point adequately will result in a loss of marks. Note also that simply saying *I would like some changes to be made to my living arrangements* is not enough to satisfy the third point in the question. What is required is an elaboration of the point, e.g. *As no meals are provided and I do not have use of a shower, I find that the situation is affecting my studies and my life in general. I sincerely hope that you will find me alternative accommodation as soon as possible. The location of the current flat is perfect for commuting to school and I would be happy if you could find me another place in this area with a toilet, a working shower and meals that meet my requirements.*

Checklist:

✓ Know the purpose of the letter and who it is for.

✓ Make sure you write in an appropriate style.

✓ Address all the points highlighted in the question adequately.

Academic and General Writing Task 2

11 Not understanding what the question is asking

It is important to read the question carefully and understand the type of task you are required to do. Look at the examples on page 24 and ask yourself the following questions.
- Which question asks for my own opinion?
- Which question asks for solutions to a problem?
- Which question asks me to present different sides of an argument?
- Which question asks me to describe causes and/or effects?

> **Example (Academic and General Writing Task 2)**
>
> **A**
> *Social media have made it easier for us to connect with other people, but some have blamed them for harming society. Discuss both the advantages and disadvantages of social media.*
>
> ---
>
> **B**
> *As result of unhealthy diets and a lack of regular exercise, obesity has become a major problem among young people. What do you think governments and schools can do to improve this situation?*
>
> ---
>
> **C**
> *The invention of the smartphone has had a direct impact on our relationships and the way we conduct business. How do you think the smartphone has changed the way we live our lives?*
>
> ---
>
> **D**
> *The focus on academic achievement in schools fails to prepare students for real life. To what extent do you agree or disagree?*

Question A requires you to see things from both points of view and discuss the different perspectives; B asks for solutions to a problem; C asks about the effects of the invention of the smartphone; D requires you to state your own opinion and justify it. In all questions, however, it is useful to consider a different point of view from your own so as to offer a balanced argument. Doing so will also help to give your own opinions greater validity.

Be careful of questions that include extreme statements, like the one in the example below.

> **Example (Academic and General Writing Task 2)**
> *The widespread availability of cheap flights and the increased ease of travelling have made it possible for us to visit places previously untouched by tourism. This can only be a good thing. Discuss.*

The sentence *This can <u>only</u> be a good thing* suggests that you should disagree with it and discuss some negative points related to tourism.

> **Tip: Answer the question**
> Do this by:
> • familiarising yourself with the question types in Task 2
> • reading the question carefully
> • writing what is required of you
> • watching out for extreme statements in the question
> • referring back to the question when writing to ensure you do not go off topic.

12 Moving from point to point without elaboration

The writer of the paragraph in the example below made several good points that are relevant to the question. However, the points were badly organised and the candidate did not explain or support the points he was making.

> **Example (Academic and General Writing Task 2)**
> *Home schooling can be good for children because they can study what they want. But some people say there is no structure for these children. Also, they will have no friends their age. But they don't need to listen to boring teachers and study subjects that are useless in real life.*

Follow up the topic sentence (your main point) with supporting evidence in the form of statistics, examples, scenarios, reasons and explanations.

> **Example (Academic and General Writing Task 2)**
> *<u>Home schooling can be good for children because they can work at their own pace and study what they want</u>. In a regular school, slower students are sometimes not able to follow lessons and feel demotivated, while faster students find the lessons boring and stop paying attention. Several homeschooled children claim that being able to choose a curriculum that suits their interests and ability helps them to learn more than the average school student.*

Checklist:

✓ Understand what the question requires you to do.

✓ Answer the question and do not go off topic.

✓ Provide supporting evidence by giving reasons, examples and explanations.

Speaking

The IELTS Speaking component takes place with a candidate and an examiner in an examination room. The test takes 11–14 minutes and has three parts.

Part 1: Introduction and overview
The examiner asks the candidate questions about familiar topics, e.g. family and friends, hobbies, favourite foods.

Part 2: Individual long turn
The examiner gives the candidate a task card with some prompts and the candidate has a minute to prepare to speak about the topic on the card. The candidate speaks for 1–2 minutes on the given topic. The examiner then follows up with one or two questions about the topic.

Part 3: Two-way discussion
The examiner asks the candidate some abstract questions related to the topic in Part 2. The candidate is required to give opinions and discuss issues.

Here are some tips for preparing yourself for the Speaking component.

- ## Focus on your breathing while you wait

  As you sit outside the examination room waiting for your name to be called, you will inevitably feel nervous. However, nervousness could have a negative effect on your ability to speak in English. Focus on your breathing and try to clear your mind as you wait. Practise tongue twisters like *Peter Piper picked a pack of pickled peppers* to loosen up the muscles of your mouth and keep stress at bay.

- ## Listen to the examiner's questions carefully

  What key words does the examiner use? What grammatical structures does he/she use in the questions? Listening for key words can help you to focus on what is required of you, while the grammatical structures could give you hints as to what tenses you should use in your answer.

- ## Let the topic bring up the vocabulary that you know

  When the examiner marks you for your lexical range, he/she is not trying to find out the entire scope of your knowledge of English vocabulary. Instead, he/she is listening to the words, phrases and collocations you use while talking about a particular topic.

  What phrases do you think might come up naturally when you are talking about your favourite restaurant? What if you were talking about healthcare in your country? Wouldn't the vocabulary set be quite different? Practise recalling relevant words and phrases for different topics.

Speaking Part 1

- ## Make sure you know enough vocabulary to talk about familiar topics

  Do you know your job title or your parents' job titles in English? Do you know the necessary vocabulary to talk about your hobby or the most important festivals in your country/town? Can you explain why you like certain types of music or films?

  The topics in Part 1 are fairly predictable, so practise talking about them and note down the key phrases that you will need to express yourself.

- ## Use the right tenses

  When you talk about your life experiences, use the present perfect tense, but switch to the past simple tense when you tell stories about the past. Use the present simple to talk about daily routines, regular occurrences and how you feel about your life and the people around you.

Speaking Part 2

- ## Make use of your one-minute preparation time wisely

  One minute is a not a long period of time, so you cannot write out your two-minute speech. Instead, use the minute to plan what you are going to say. Use the following question words to guide you: *Who? What? Where? When? Why? How?*

Example (Speaking Part 2)
Talk about a present that you received.

Ask yourself the following questions and note down key words and phrases that would help you answer them.

o Who gave you the present?
o What was it? Describe it. What is it used for?
o Where did you receive it? What happened when you opened the present?
o When did you receive it?
o Why did the person give you this present?
o How did you feel when you received it? How do you feel about it now?

For some tasks, *Why?* and *How?* might be more important than *Who?* or *When?*, while in others, *Who?* might be the most important point to elaborate on. Decide what is most important by referring to the question, and elaborate on that first.

- ## Do not forget to describe smells, sounds and feelings

  Whether you are describing a visit to a market you love or meeting a person you admire for the first time, it is natural to focus on appearances and events. However, you can add interest and depth to your description by including information about sounds, smells and feelings, e.g. *The moment I entered the market, I was overwhelmed by the number of stalls there. Vendors were yelling and trying to sell everything from plates to old books and clothes. I sniffed the sweet smell of soy sauce and fried noodles coming from the food stalls and I instantly felt hungry. The atmosphere was electric and although the weather was hot and humid, I felt excited and energised.*

  If you have trouble remembering or recounting the details of an event, close your eyes and visualise it. Try to recall all the sensations you experienced. The more often you practise visualising events, the more easily you will be able to do it. Use this visualisation technique in the test if necessary to help yourself focus.

- ## Record yourself talking

  Practise planning your talk in one minute and then speaking for 2 minutes. Record yourself and play back the recording. Listen out for areas you can improve on and also good use of language and clear descriptions.

Speaking Part 3

- ## Give your opinions, but be balanced

  Show the examiner that you can see things from different points of view by offering a counter-argument to your own point of view. Use phrases like *On the other hand, Conversely, Others might argue that ...* to signal an alternative viewpoint.

- ## Display your ability to use complex grammatical structures

  Part 3 offers you the chance to talk about more abstract subjects and therefore the opportunity to use hypotheticals like the second and third conditional. You could also use modals to express possibility, make suggestions and predictions.

Common errors

Here are some common mistakes that candidates make when doing the Speaking component. You should be aware of these pitfalls as you prepare for the exam. The following points apply to all three parts of the Speaking component, although examples are taken from particular parts.

1   Giving short answers to all questions

Example (Speaking Part 1)	
Examiner:	*Do you celebrate any traditional holidays with your family?*
Candidate A:	*Yes. Chinese New Year.*
Examiner:	*And what do you do during Chinese New Year?*
Candidate A:	*I have dinner with my family.*
Examiner:	*Do you celebrate any traditional holidays with your family?*
Candidate B:	*Yes, I do. Every year on New Year's Eve, my family gets together for a big dinner and we welcome the Chinese New Year with festive songs and fireworks. There's a belief that if we stay up late, ...*

Candidate A gave very short answers and therefore was unable to demonstrate fluency. She also missed the opportunity to demonstrate her lexical and grammatical range. Short answers could greatly affect your speaking score, so try to expand on them. Candidate B's answer does this by giving some good details.

Now look at the example below. Candidate C expands on her answer by explaining and giving reasons and examples to clarify what she is saying.

Example (Speaking Part 3)	
Examiner:	*Do you think sports bring people together?*
Candidate C:	*Yes, I do. When there are important sporting events like the Olympics or the World Cup, people often gather to watch the events or games together. They experience the same emotions: they laugh and they cry together. These experiences can really bring people together.*

Tip: Demonstrate fluency
Do this by:
- describing a scenario
- explaining and giving reasons
- using examples to clarify what you are saying.

2   Repeating the same vocabulary too often

Example (Speaking Part 2)	
Question:	*Describe a place you visited and that you really loved.*
Candidate D:	*... The market was very nice and, er ... I liked going there. And I liked going with my friend. It was a very nice experience. My friend thought it was nice too.*

Using the same basic vocabulary over and over again demonstrates to the examiner that you have a limited range of vocabulary, and this could cost you marks. You should try to use as wide a range of vocabulary as possible. You can also use synonyms, paraphrase or describe something in more detail, as in the example on page 29. Practise doing this whenever you have a chance to speak English. Find alternatives for words that people over-use, like *nice, good, bad, interesting, enjoy, like, hate, very* and *really*. How many alternatives does Candidate E use for *nice*?

Example (Speaking Part 2)

Question: *Describe a place you visited and that you really loved.*

Candidate E: *... The market was amazing and I had a wonderful time. It was full of people and so busy and noisy, but I didn't mind it at all because it just added to the atmosphere. There were hundreds of stalls selling a whole range of objects, from arts and crafts to clothes and mobile phone accessories. And there was more food than I had ever seen before. My friend came with me and it was great being able to share the experience with her.*

Although it is best not to over-use the same words, you can occasionally repeat a point you are trying to make. You could refer back to what you have previously said in order to make your point clearer and stronger by using phrases like *As I said before, ...* and *Coming back to what I was saying earlier, ...* .

Tip: Show your range of vocabulary

Do this by:

• using synonyms
• paraphrasing what you have already said if you need to say it again
• describing something in more detail.

3   Trying to answer a question you do not understand

Example (Speaking Part 3)

Examiner: *What can developed countries do about the poverty in developing countries?*

Candidate F: *Yeah, I think ... Well, developed countries can do ... um ... do more poverty in developing countries.*

You cannot avoid answering a question simply by repeating it back to the examiner. If you do not understand the question, do not be afraid to ask for repetition or clarification.

Useful phrases: Asking for clarification

I'm sorry. I'm not sure what you mean by 'poverty'.
Do you mind clarifying that for me?
I'm afraid I didn't quite catch that. Could you repeat the question, please?

4   Learning prepared answers

Avoid memorising paragraphs and long sentences. Candidates who prepare answers are often so concerned with trying to remember their prepared answers that they fail to pay attention to the question and end up using their prepared answers in the wrong context. Remember that examiners are trained to detect memorised answers and you could be penalised for giving an answer you have learnt by heart. Instead, when preparing for the test, learn some key phrases and practise talking about different topics. Remember the good points you made or the interesting examples you gave. And when speaking to the examiner, be yourself and speak naturally.

5   Overusing linking words and fixed adverbial phrases

Some candidates think that the more linking words/phrases and adverbials they use, the higher their score. Consequently, they use as many of these as they can, filling a short speech with words and phrases like *nevertheless, in spite of the fact that, what's more*, and *as far as I'm concerned*. Linking words/phrases and adverbials should clarify what you say, help you to organise your points and help your listener to understand you easily. They should fit the content and not stand out from it. Inappropriate usage can prevent you from getting a higher IELTS score.

Checklist:

✓ Expand your answers by giving details, examples and explanations.

✓ Demonstrate your range of vocabulary by using synonyms and by paraphrasing, and by describing things in more detail.

✓ If you do not understand a question, ask the examiner to repeat the question or clarify a word.

✓ Speak from the heart. Do not memorise prepared answers.

✓ Use linking words/phrases and adverbials appropriately to make what you say clearer.

Test 1

SECTION 1   *Questions 1–10*

Questions 1–3

Choose the correct letter, A, B or C.

Example
The customer is leaving from
  A Main Street.
  B Centenary Square.
  C Central Bus Station.

1 The customer's coach departs at
  A 1.00 p.m. •
  B 2.00 p.m.
  C 3.00 p.m.

2 The customer wants
  A a single ticket. •
  B a return ticket.
  C an open return ticket.

3 The customer is going to London
  A to attend a family party.
  B to see his daughter.
  C for a meeting.

Questions 4–7

Complete the notes below.

*Write **NO MORE THAN TWO WORDS** or **A NUMBER** for each answer.*

Kieren Coaches

Name:	Matthew (4) _____
Address:	34 (5) _____ Aulaslay Road
Telephone:	01732 (6) _____
Email:	matt (7) _____ @yahoo.co.uk

Questions 8–10

*Choose the correct letter, **A, B** or **C**.*

8 Apart from hand luggage, travellers

    A must pay £10 for luggage.

    B can only take two additional suitcases.

    C are allowed up to 40 kilos of luggage free of charge.

9 Travel insurance

    A is included.

    B costs extra.

    C is compulsory.

10 The customer decides to pay

    A by debit card.

    B in cash.

    C by cheque.

SECTION 2   *Questions 11–20*

02

Questions 11–13

Choose THREE letters, A–F.

Which **THREE** changes have been made to the library over the summer?

    A a new roof

    B new computers

    C new shelf units

    D a self-service system

    E meeting room decorated

    F new furniture for the children

Questions 14–16

Write NO MORE THAN THREE WORDS for each answer.

Which **THREE** events does the speaker say are taking place in September?

14 _____

15 _____

16 _____

Questions 17–18

Choose the correct letter, A, B or C.

17 The library needs a teacher for the Computer Club because

    A the current teacher is leaving.

    B they are starting an additional group.

    C they want to start a higher-level class.

18 Who does the library want older people to talk to about the past?

    A teachers

    B young children

    C teenagers

Questions 19–20

Choose TWO letters A–E.

In addition to books, which two services does the mobile library offer?

    A computer lessons

    B a reservation service

    C a reference section

    D newspapers and magazines

    E community advice

SECTION 3   *Questions 21–30*

03

Questions 21–23

Complete the sentences below.

Write NO MORE THAN THREE WORDS for each answer.

21 The best days for engineering students are _____.

22 Students can get useful suggestions about _____.

23 Use the internet to look at _____ before the event.

Questions 24–27

Choose the correct letter, A, B or C.

24 Fergus says that
    A there is one company he is particularly interested in.
    B he has done some research already.
    C he knows the boss at one of the companies.

25 The tutor thinks Fergus should
    A prepare questions in advance.
    B research the skills required for jobs before the event.
    C find out what the starting salaries are.

26 Fergus plans
    A to wear a suit and tie.
    B to wear smart but casual clothes.
    C to buy an outfit for the event.

27 The tutor suggests that Fergus
    A should ask particular people certain questions.
    B should avoid taking free gifts.
    C should treat conversations like short interviews.

Questions 28–30

Choose THREE letters A–F.

Why do the tutor and Fergus think it is useful to attend a jobs fair?

    A to get a job

    B to find out what employers want from you

    C to give employers your contact details

    D to discover which are the key companies to work for

    E to practise your communication skills

    F to make useful contacts

SECTION 4   Questions 31–40

04

Questions 31–33

Choose the correct letter, A, B or C.

31 According to the speaker,
- **A** people were healthier in the past.
- **B** ancient bones need to be handled with care.
- **C** bones offer clues to a person's lifestyle.

32 The island of Vanuatu
- **A** was not always inhabited.
- **B** had no food sources.
- **C** was the only island in Remote Oceania.

33 Archaeologists wanted to discover
- **A** what resources were available on the island.
- **B** if the settlers could rely entirely on local food sources.
- **C** the extent to which the settlers ate food they had brought with them.

Questions 34–37

Complete the sentences below.

*Write **NO MORE THAN THREE WORDS** for each answer.*

34 Bones provide a dietary _____ of the things people ate.

35 Different ratios of carbon and sulphur are found in organisms depending on whether they come from the _____.

36 Archaeologists analysed modern and _____ food sources for chemical elements.

37 The settlers ate wild creatures as well as _____.

Questions 38–39

Choose TWO letters, A–D.

An analysis of the bones of men and women suggest that

    A females ate more meat than males.

    B diet could have been determined by the job the person did.

    C some people held higher status than others.

    D food was distributed equally amongst the settlers.

Question 40

Choose the correct letter, A, B or C.

The bones of pigs and chickens indicate that these animals

    A only ate food provided by the settlers.

    B were a main source of food for the settlers.

    C probably did not consume the settlers' limited food supplies.

READING

READING PASSAGE 1

*You should spend about 20 minutes on **Questions 1–14**, which are based on Reading Passage 1 below.*

Questions 1–5

*Reading Passage 1 has six paragraphs, **A–F**.*

*Choose the correct heading for paragraphs **B–F** from the list of headings below.*

*Write the correct number, **i–ix**, next to Questions 1–5.*

List of Headings
i   What are metabolites?
ii   The negative effects of allelopathy
iii Biological warfare in the plant world
iv   Why we cannot use allelopathic chemicals at present
v   What is allelopathy?
vi   The reasons why plants compete with other plants
vii The effects of allelopathy and realisation of its possible uses
viii How could we use allelopathic chemicals in farming?
ix   Specific examples of allelopathic plants

Example	Answer
Paragraph **A**	iii

1   Paragraph **B**
2   Paragraph **C**
3   Paragraph **D**
4   Paragraph **E**
5   Paragraph **F**

Mutual harm

A In forests and fields all over the world, plants are engaged in a deadly chemical war to suppress other plants and create conditions for their own success. But what if we could learn the secrets of these plants and use them for our own purposes? Would it be possible to use their strategies and weapons to help us improve agriculture by preventing weeds from germinating and encouraging growth in crops? This possibility is leading agricultural researchers to explore the effects plants have on other plants with the aim of applying their findings to farming.

B The phenomenon by which an organism produces one or more chemicals that influence the growth, survival and reproduction of other organisms is called allelopathy. These chemicals are a subset of chemicals produced by organisms called secondary metabolites. A plant's primary metabolites are associated with growth and development. Allelochemicals, however, are part of a plant's defence system and have a secondary function in the life of the organism. The term *allelopathy* comes from the Greek: *allelo* and *pathy* meaning 'mutual harm'. The term was first used by the Austrian scientist Hans Molisch in 1937, but people have been noting the negative effects that one plant can have on another for a long time. In 300 BC, the Greek philosopher Theophrastus noticed that pigweed had a negative effect on alfalfa plants. In China, around the first century AD, the author of *Shennong Ben Cao Jing* described 267 plants that have the ability to kill pests.

C Allelopathy can be observed in many aspects of plant ecology. It can affect where certain species of plants grow, the fertility of competitor plants, the natural change of plant communities over time, which plant species are able to dominate a particular area, and the diversity of plants in an area. Plants can release allelopathic chemicals in several ways: their roots can release chemicals directly into the soil, and their bark and leaves can release chemicals into the soil as they rot. Initially, scientists were interested in the negative effects of allelopathic chemicals. Observations of the phenomenon included poor growth of some forest trees, damage to crops, changes in vegetation patterns and, interestingly, the occurrence of weed-free areas. It was also realised that some species could have beneficial effects on agricultural crop plants and the possible application of allelopathy became the subject of research.

D Today research is focused on the effects of weeds on crops, the effects of crops on weeds, and how certain crops affect other crops. Agricultural scientists are exploring the use of allelochemicals to regulate growth and to act as natural herbicides, thereby promoting sustainable agriculture by using these natural chemicals as an alternative to man-made chemicals. For example, a small fast-growing tree found in Central America, sometimes called the 'miracle tree', contains a poison that slows the growth of other trees but does not affect its own seeds. Chemicals produced by this tree have been shown to improve the production of rice. Similarly, box elder – another tree – stimulates the growth of bluestem grass, which is a tall prairie grass found in the mid-western United States. Many weeds may use allelopathy to become ecologically successful; a study in China found that 25 out of 33 highly poisonous weeds had significant allelopathic properties.

E   There may be at least three applications of allelopathy to agriculture. Firstly, the allelopathic properties of wild or cultivated plants may be bred into crop plants through genetic modification or traditional breeding methods to improve the release of desired allelochemicals and thus improve crop yield. Secondly, a plant with strong allelopathic properties could be used to control weeds by planting it in rotation with an agricultural crop and then leaving it to rot and become part of the soil in order to inhibit the growth of weeds. Finally, naturally occurring allelopathic chemicals could be used in combination with man-made chemicals. Boosting the efficiency of man-made herbicides could lead to a reduction in the amount of herbicides used in agriculture, which is better for the environment.

F   Despite the promising uses of allelopathic chemicals, agricultural scientists are still cautious. Firstly, allelopathic chemicals may break down and disappear in the soil more easily than artificial chemicals. Secondly, allelopathic chemicals may be harmful to plants other than weeds. Thirdly, allelopathic chemicals could persist in the soil for a long time and may affect crops grown in the same field as the allelopathic plants at a later date. Because the effects of allelopathic chemicals are not yet fully known, agricultural scientists will need to continue to study the biological war between plants.

Questions 6–9

Choose the correct letter, A, B, C or D.

6   What does the term 'allelopathy' refer to?

   A   the growth and development of a plant

   B   the relationship between plants that grown in the same area

   C   the effects of chemicals produced by a plant on another plant

   D   a plant's primary metabolic processes

7   Which of the following does allelopathy NOT affect?

   A   how certain species of plants change the nature of the soil where they grow

   B   the diversity of plants in an area

   C   the nutrients present in the soil

   D   the location in which plants can grow

8   Scientists are mainly interested in

   A   being able to exploit allelopathy in sustainable farming.

   B   the beneficial effects of weeds on crops.

   C   the effect of allelopathy on forests.

   D   the negative effects of weeds.

9   Which of the following is NOT mentioned in the text?

   A   a tree which is highly poisonous to weeds

   B   a tree which makes a type of grass grow better

   C   a tree which makes rice more productive

   D   a tree which produces a chemical that affects the growth of other trees

Questions 10–14

Complete the summary of paragraphs E and F below.

*Choose **NO MORE THAN TWO WORDS** from the passage for each answer.*

Write your answers in spaces 10–14.

Scientists can see three potential uses of allelopathic chemicals in farming. Firstly, the ability to produce allelopathic chemicals could be **(10)** _____bred_____ into agricultural crops; secondly, allelopathic plants could be planted in rotation with the **(11)** _____[growth of weeds]_____; finally, naturally produced chemicals could be combined with **(12)** _____man-made_____ herbicides. However, agriculturalists are still **(13)** _____cautious_____ as allelopathic plants may have negative effects on plants which are not the intended target and the chemicals could remain in the ground for a(n) **(14)** _____long time_____, even after the plants themselves have died.

[handwritten annotation in margin: agricultural crop]

*You should spend about 20 minutes on **Questions 15–26**, which are based on Reading Passage 2 below.*

Ordinary treasures

When Andy Warhol, one of the twentieth century's most influential artists, died his four-floor house was so full of items that the only rooms you could walk through were the kitchen and the bedroom. It turned out that Warhol had compulsive hoarding disorder, which is defined as the excessive accumulation of objects and a refusal to throw them away. But Warhol's case is not uncommon; around five per cent of Americans – nearly 15 million people – suffer from compulsive hoarding disorder. This disorder interferes with daily activities such as sleeping and cooking, and in an extreme form it can harm one's health, be a fire risk and even lead to death. Although researchers suspect that the disorder is more widespread in the West, cases of hoarding have been recorded in almost every country.

Twenty years ago, compulsive hoarding disorder was a relatively unexplored psychological phenomenon, often treated as an aspect of obsessive compulsive disorder – the compulsion to repeat a certain action over and over. However, it is now recognised as a separate disorder. Scientists from many disciplines, including psychologists, neurologists and behavioural researchers are looking at gene sequences within hoarders' DNA and scanning their brains to try to understand their behaviour in the hope that they can be helped.

There are several theories for the behaviour. First of all, hoarding appears to run in families and may have genetic causes, with family members often having similar issues. In a study of 219 families, researchers at Johns Hopkins University found that families with two or more hoarding members showed a linkage between hoarding behaviour and chromosome 14 – one of the 23 pairs of chromosomes that make up human DNA. A second theory states that the instinct to hoard may be an evolutionary survival strategy: there are plenty of examples of hoarding in the animal kingdom. The Arctic gray jay hoards around 100,000 berries and insects so that it has enough food for the long winter months. Humans, however, are the only species that take the strategy to extremes, sometimes filling their homes with so many objects that they eventually become uninhabitable.

Recent psychological research, however, emphasises that hoarders do not just collect junk; nor are they lazy or disorganised, even if their homes are chaotic. Many hoarders have normal lives, with regular jobs and normal relationships with friends and family. Cognitively, hoarders tend to be emotional, attaching sentimental value to belongings that other people would discard. They also tend to be intelligent, well educated and more creative than average. However, they can be indecisive and may start several different projects at the same time.

Carol Mathews, a leading researcher into the condition, used magnetic resonance imaging (MRI) to show brain activity in the process of decision making. People with compulsive hoarding disorder display increased activity in an area of the brain related to decision making when asked to organise objects. This increased activity is due to their greater emotional attachment to possessions. In other tests, Mathews found that people with hoarding behaviour had difficulty grouping similar objects and remembering the sequence of things. In effect, people with compulsive hoarding disorder do not categorise objects in the same way as other people, and when they are asked to do so, show an increase in brain activity associated with the decision-making process. It seems that people with hoarding behaviour see and treat objects differently and might have a different appreciation of the physical world. For example, a pile of objects in the middle of a room may be seen as a work of art by a hoarder rather than just a heap of junk.

Treating hoarding effectively may depend upon whether we can identify specific character traits. Dr Monika Eckfield of the University of California, San Francisco, believes there are two different kinds of people with hoarding behaviour. She calls one kind impulsive-acquirers, who buy objects out of excitement and keep them because they are interested in them. The other type are the worried-keepers – the hoarders who acquire items passively and keep them in case they need them in future. Worried-keepers spend more time sorting and organising belongings. While both kinds of hoarders of either gender find it nearly impossible to throw anything away, more men than women belong to the former category whilst more women fall into the worried-keeper group.

QUESTIONS 15–19

Do the following statements agree with the information given in Reading Passage 2?
Write

> **TRUE**   *if the statement agrees with the information*
> **FALSE**   *if the statement contradicts the information*
> **NOT GIVEN**   *if there is no information on this*

15 People have died as a result of extreme hoarding behaviour.

16 Compulsive hoarding disorder is a type of obsessive compulsive disorder.

17 People with compulsive hoarding disorder usually have parents with the same condition.

18 People who take collecting to extremes eventually cannot live in their homes.

19 Hoarders show more activity in parts of the brain associated with the emotions.

Questions 20–25

Classify the following as typical of

    A *impulsive-acquirer hoarders*

    B *worried-keeper hoarders*

    C *both*

*Write the correct letter, **A**, **B** or **C**, next to Questions 20–25.*

20 This type of hoarder finds it almost impossible to discard anything. *C*

21 This type of hoarder keeps possessions because he/she finds them interesting. *B ~ A*

22 This type of hoarder keeps objects for future use. *B*

23 This type of hoarder buys things because he/she is excited by them. *A A*

24 This type of hoarder has a greater tendency to sort objects. *B*

25 This type of hoarder includes more men than women. *A*

Question 26

*Choose the correct letter, **A**, **B** or **C**.*

The writer of the article views people with compulsive hoarding disorder as

    A lazy and disorganised.

    B abnormal because they cannot lead a normal life.

    C having a different perception of physical objects from the majority of people.

READING PASSAGE 3

*You should spend about 20 minutes on **Questions 27–40**, which are based on Reading Passage 3 below.*

A A major cause of blindness in the industrialised world is age-related macular degeneration (AMD). It affects approximately three million people globally and accounts for around nine per cent of all blindness. These statistics are expected to double by the year 2020 as the world population increases. Scientists have been working on a new treatment for one type of the disease by using stem cells to repair damage to the retina, with positive results. Two women in America, both registered as blind, were given the new treatment and say their vision improved just weeks after they were injected with the stems cells. With such promising results for a condition which previously had no treatment, researchers are positive about the direction of the stem cell treatment.

B AMD usually affects the elderly although younger people can also develop a version of the condition. People with AMD typically have dark patches at the centre of their vision – the deterioration takes place over months and years. Although people with AMD do not lose their sight completely, they do lose central vision, which is vital for detailed work and activities like reading and driving, so that leading a normal life can become impossible over time. In the cases of the two American women, one was a graphic artist who began to lose her vision in her twenties. As she lost most of her central vision, she became unable to work, and then eventually it became impossible for her to recognise people or watch TV. The second woman became unable to recognise faces, had to stop driving and in the end could not leave her home.

C To understand AMD, we need to understand how our eyes work. Essentially a hollow ball, the eye has a number of layers. The outer layer consists of the white of the eye and the cornea. The cornea is the transparent area in front of the coloured iris and the black pupil at the centre of the iris. The middle layer of the eye includes blood vessels and the iris, which regulates the amount of light entering the eye. Just behind the iris is the lens, which focuses images on the retina, which covers the inside of the eyeball. The retina is the part of the eye that contains photoreceptors – cells that sense light. Nerve fibres from the photoreceptors in the retina join together to form the optic nerve, which then exits the eyeball and transmits visual information to the brain. The photoreceptors are of two types, rods and cones: the rods are sensitive to light intensity and the cones are sensitive to colour. They are mostly concentrated in the part of the retina called the macula. This is only the size of a grain of rice, but it is responsible for our central vision, most of our colour vision and our visual acuity, or sharpness of vision. The photoreceptor cells lie on a thin layer of cells that provide them with nutrients and carry away waste. When these underlying cells die or are damaged, the photoreceptor cells cannot function properly, and this leads to a loss of vision.

D Damage to the macula can result from a variety of factors. Age is the main risk factor but smoking also damages blood vessels and the structure of the eye. Smokers are three times more likely to develop AMD, as are people with poor diets. A diet lacking in fruit and vegetables cannot help the body defend itself against free radical molecules which damage cells. Fruit and vegetables contain antioxidants, which protect the body against these free radicals. Finally, people with high blood pressure are one and a half times more likely to contract AMD, as are those people with a family history of the disease.

E The new treatment for AMD, developed by Dr Robert Lanza at Advanced Cell Technology, involves changing embryonic stem cells into more specialised eye stem cells and injecting 50,000 of them into the layer of the eye that supports the photoreceptors. A stem cell is a primary cell that has the ability to divide and form specialised cells that perform various functions within the body. First, a single stem cell was taken from a human embryo and grown into a colony of millions of cells. The cells were checked to make sure they were healthy. Then another procedure encouraged the stem cells to develop into the type of cell that forms the layer under the photoreceptor cells. The eye stem cells were injected below the retina through a cut into the eyeball, where they filled in the gaps left by dead and damaged cells and began functioning again.

F For the two patients, the results have been stunning. Tests have indicated that healthy cells have grown where the stem cells were injected. The first woman has regained enough vision to be able to cycle. Meanwhile, the second woman can read, cook and go shopping by herself again. The hope is that the treatment could be a way forward for other currently incurable conditions so that other people can lead normal lives again.

Questions 27–32

Reading Passage 3 has six paragraphs, A–F.

Which paragraphs, A–F, contain the following information?

Write the correct letter, A–F, next to Questions 27–32.

27 the symptoms of AMD
28 details about the treatment process
29 factors that may contribute to AMD
30 the physical causes of AMD
31 potential future uses of stem cell treatment
32 the frequency of occurrence of AMD

Questions 33–35

Label the diagram below using words from the box.

> macula
> cornea
> optic nerve

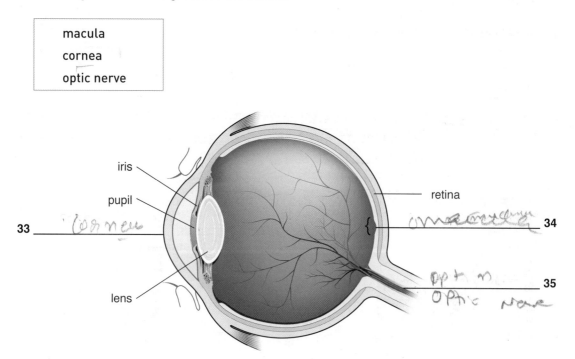

iris

pupil

retina

33 _____ *cornea*

34 *macula*

35 *opt n* / *optic nerve*

lens

Questions 36–40

Complete the summary below.

*Choose **NO MORE THAN TWO WORDS** from the passage for each answer.*

Write your answers in spaces 36–40.

Age-related macular degeneration (AMD) is one of the main causes of loss of sight in the *In Industrialised World*
(36) _____ *younger people*. Although AMD can affect **(37)** _____ *three millions*, the
majority of sufferers are older. Despite being very small, the macula is essential to our
(38) _____ *Central vision* as well as detailed vision and some colour vision. AMD happens
when the cells beneath the **(39)** _____ *Underlying* *Retina* cells are damaged or die. A new
treatment to repair the damaged cells involves **(40)** _____ *Injecting* 50,000 stem cells
under the retina, after which they regenerate the damaged area. *Changing cells*

WRITING TASK 1

You should spend about 20 minutes on this task.

> The graphs below show the growth in wages within the G7 nations between 2000–2007 and 2008–2012.
>
> Summarise the information by selecting and reporting the main features, and make comparisons where relevant.

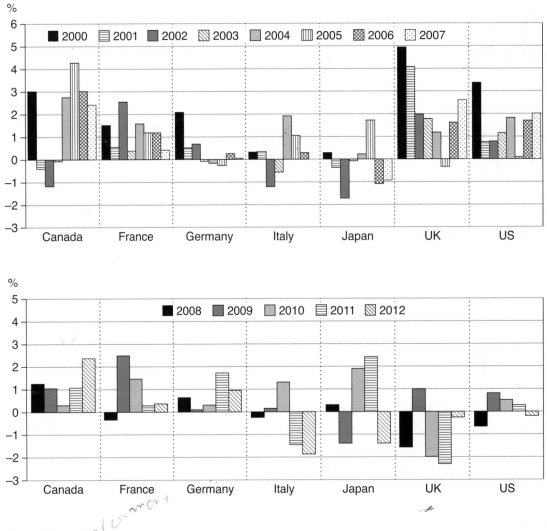

Write at least 150 words.

WRITING TASK 2

You should spend about 40 minutes on this task.

Write about the following topic:

> The car is possibly the most convenient and popular way of getting from A
> to B. However, due to its impact on the environment and the risk it poses to
> pedestrians and motorists, governments should take urgent steps to reduce
> our dependency on this mode of transport.
>
> To what extent do you agree or disagree?

Give reasons for your answer and include any relevant examples from your own knowledge
or experience.

Write at least 250 words.

Positive —   easy convay to reach

PART 1: Introduction and interview

Listen to Track 05, pressing pause after each question to answer.

05

PART 2: Individual long turn

Before you read the task card, listen to Track 06.

06

> Describe a moment in your life when you were very excited.
>
> You should say
>
>   when this was
>
>   what you were excited about
>
>   what eventually happened
>
> and say what it was about this moment that makes it so memorable.

PART 3: Two-way discussion

Listen to Track 07, pressing pause after each question to answer.

07

Test 2

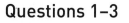

LISTENING

SECTION 1   *Questions 1–10*

Questions 1–3

Choose the correct letter, A, B or C.

> *Example*
>
> Jason says the house
>
> **A** ~~is close to the university.~~
> **B** is in the student area of town.
> **C** is near a bus service to the university.

1 Katie thought the house

     A would be too small for them.
     B would be quite cheap.
     C would not be like the advertisement claimed.

2 Jason says

     A Katie's parents would like the house.
     B there is no communal area in the house.
     C the house needs decorating.

3 Jason likes the landlady because

     A she used to be a student herself.
     B she has a lot of properties.
     C she takes care of the house.

Questions 4–6

Choose THREE letters, A–G.

Which THREE of the following do the house and its vicinity have?

A   a garden

B   a washing machine

C   an internet connection

D   parking restrictions

E   a modern kitchen

F   a garage

G   local shops

Questions 7–10

Complete the notes below.

Write NO MORE THAN THREE WORDS or A NUMBER for each answer.

RENT DETAILS

Address: 94 (7) _____

Monthly rent: (8) £ _____

                                      (9) _____ rent to be paid as deposit

Telephone number: 01764 (10) _____

09

SECTION 2   *Questions 11–20*

Questions 11–13

*Choose the correct letter, **A, B** or **C**.*

11 When Amanda was bitten,

    A she felt a sharp pain in her foot.

    B she believed she was in serious trouble.

    C she started to shake all over.

12 Amanda

    A checked to see if there was anything in her shoes first.

    B found a fault in one of her shoes.

    C was aware of common ways of getting bitten.

13 When Tony saw the spider,

    A he picked it up.

    B he hit it with Amanda's shoe.

    C he covered it with a glass container.

Questions 14–15

Complete the sentences below.

*Write **NO MORE THAN TWO WORDS** for each answer.*

FIRST AID ADVICE

Place a(n) **(14)** _____ over the bite to relieve the pain.

Do not place a(n) **(15)** _____ over the bite as this can cause further pain.

Questions 16–18

Choose THREE letters, A–E.

Which **THREE** symptoms did Amanda have before going into hospital?

- **A** a painful lower leg
- **B** feeling sick
- **C** a fever
- **D** a headache
- **E** swelling

Questions 19–20

Complete the sentences below.

*Write **NO MORE THAN TWO WORDS** or **A NUMBER** for each answer.*

19 Following treatment, symptoms can sometimes take a few _____ to clear up.

20 Amanda flew home _____ later.

SECTION 3   *Questions 21–30*

Questions 21–25

*Choose the correct letter, **A**, **B** or **C**.*

21 Kevin has lectures

    A three days a week.

    B on Wednesdays.

    C four days a week.

22 What does Kevin say about going home?

    A He last went home in September.

    B It is too expensive to travel by train.

    C He has been back home once.

23 Kevin thinks living in halls of residence

    A is cheaper than renting a house.

    B is a good way of getting to know people.

    C means it is difficult to use the kitchen.

24 Kevin joined the Spanish Society because

    A he wanted to learn how to cook.

    B someone told him it was good.

    C he knows people who are members.

25 The tutor says it is important for students to structure their time because

    A they have more independence at university.

    B they have too much free time.

    C it is the best way to get top grades in their work.

Questions 26–30

Complete the sentences below.

Write **NO MORE THAN THREE WORDS** *or* **A NUMBER** *for each answer.*

Writing Tutorial Service

Get feedback on your academic writing skills!

Send us a piece of work along with a completed **(26)** _____.

The team may not be familiar with your subject, so try one of the general
(27) _____ you will find on our webpage.

When applying for a tutorial, tell us when you are **(28)** _____.

We usually arrange to see you within **(29)** _____ of receiving
your application.

Under normal circumstances, students will be able to meet the team once every
(30) _____.

SECTION 4   *Questions 31–40*

🎧
11

Questions 31–32

Choose the correct letter, A, B or C.

31 According to the speaker, which of the following models emerged first?

   A equity-based crowdfunding

   B micro-lending

   C fan-based crowdfunding

32 The fan-based model offers

   A shares.

   B a financial return.

   C a reward.

Questions 33–40

Complete the sentences below.

Write **NO MORE THAN TWO WORDS** *for each answer.*

Crowdfunding explained

- The project and financial target are explained on the crowdfunding website.
- Each fundraising initiative has a set **(33)** _____ limit.
- For a film, people could expect anything from free tickets to having their name listed in the **(34)** _____.

Crowdfunding opportunities

- Companies can receive small donations from a(n) **(35)** _____ of people.
- Partner companies can help as part of their own fundraising events.
- You can get **(36)** _____ from supporters during the development phase.
- Crowdfunding will increase **(37)** _____ of the product and potentially improve sales.

Crowdfunding dangers

- You must reach your target or donations are **(38)** _____.
- It can take a lot of time to fulfil the promises you have made to fans.
- Don't forget to consider the cost of **(39)** _____ when working out profits.
- Raising awareness is hard if your company is **(40)** _____ or if you don't have many social media followers.

READING PASSAGE 1

*You should spend about 20 minutes on **Questions 1–13**, which are based on Reading Passage 1 below.*

The Humungous Fungus

If you were asked what is the largest organism in the world, what would your answer be? A blue whale or a redwood tree? Or perhaps a giant squid? You would be wrong. But this is understandable because the world's largest organism is largely hidden from sight and was discovered only relatively recently in 1998 in the soil of Oregon's Blue Mountains. It is a fungus nearly ten square kilometres in area and one metre deep. It may be not only the largest single organism in the world but also one of the oldest. Based on its current rate of growth, the fungus is thought to be around 2,400 years old; however, it is also possible that it has been growing for the past 8,650 years. Commonly known as the honey mushroom, the only visible evidence for the organism on the surface is groups of golden mushrooms that grow in forests during the autumn.

The discovery of the organism came about when Catherine Parks, a scientist at the Pacific Northwest Research Station in Oregon, heard about trees dying from root rot in a forest east of Prairie City. Using aerial photographs, she identified an area of dying trees stretching over a 5.6 kilometre area. She then collected samples from the roots of these trees. When she looked at the samples, Parks was able to confirm that many of the samples were infected by the same organism; the fungus had grown bigger than any other creature known to science. A combination of good genes and stable conditions has enabled it to spread. In addition, the dry climate of the region makes it difficult for new fungi to establish themselves and compete with established fungi.

The technique for identifying the fungus was developed in 1992, when the first gigantic fungus was discovered in Michigan. A PhD biology student, Myron Smith, discovered it in a hardwood forest, when he and his team were trying to find the boundaries of individual fungi. After a year of testing, they still had not found the boundary of a particular fungus. The next thing they did was develop new genetic tests to see if the DNA from the samples was from a single individual fungus and not closely related individuals. Eventually, they realised that they had found a 1,500-year-old fungus that weighed over 90 metric tonnes.

The honey mushroom fungus is the cause of a root disease that kills many trees in the US and Canada. It has fine filaments or tubes that grow along tree roots and connect together to form a mat. The mat then slowly consumes the food source: it produces chemicals that digest carbohydrates from the tree and interfere with the tree's ability to absorb water and nutrients, eventually leading to the death of the host organism. As well as producing feeding filaments, the honey fungus is able to spread by producing string-like growths that reach out to find new potential food sources. The fungus spreads very slowly over hundreds of years, seeking out food and killing its victims. Not surprisingly, forest service scientists are interested in learning to control the fungus but they also realise that it has an important role to play in the forest's ecology.

Fungi have both beneficial and harmful effects. They are essential because they decompose or break down waste matter on the forest floor and recycle nutrients. They are also central to many processes that are important to humans: they are vital to the process of making many kinds of food, including cheese, bread and wine. They have been used in the production of medicines, and particularly antibiotics. Even the golden mushrooms produced by the honey mushroom fungus are edible, though apparently not very tasty. On the other hand, fungi also form a major group of organisms harmful to plants and animals. Some mushrooms produced by fungi, such as the death cap mushroom and the fool's mushroom, are extremely poisonous to humans. Fungi can spoil food which has been stored, and of course they can kill trees and other plants.

Although to humans the idea of an enormous organism silently growing underground seems very strange, Tom Volk, a biology professor at the University of Wisconsin-La Crosse, explains that this may be in the nature of things for a fungus. 'We think that these things are not very rare,' he says. 'We think that they're in fact normal.'

Questions 1–7

Do the following statements agree with the information given in Reading Passage 1?

Write

TRUE	if the statement agrees with the information
FALSE	if the statement contradicts the information
NOT GIVEN	if there is no information on this

1 The fungus is perhaps the world's oldest living organism.

2 Catherine Parks wanted to work in Oregon.

3 Photos taken from the air helped her to locate the fungus.

4 Myron Smith developed a test to see which organisms are related to fungi.

5 The fungus damages trees by digesting carbohydrates that are part of the tree.

6 The mushrooms from the honey mushroom fungus are poisonous to humans.

7 The fungi are the largest group of organisms harmful to humans.

Questions 8–13

Complete the summary below.

Choose **NO MORE THAN TWO WORDS** from the passage for each answer.

Write your answers in spaces 8–13.

The largest known organism is a fungus, the only **(8)** _____ signs of which are mushrooms which appear in autumn. The fungus was discovered when a scientist was studying **(9)** _____ across a large area of forest in Oregon. The fungus is responsible for a(n) **(10)** _____ that kills the trees. Scientists determined that the fungus was a single organism by using **(11)** _____ to see if DNA samples were from the same individual. Although the concept of an enormous organism living **(12)** _____ is strange to humans, scientists think it may be **(13)** _____.

2:15

You should spend about 20 minutes on Questions 14–26, which are based on Reading Passage 2 below.

models

Theory

Style Shifting

A How do we recognise an individual's personal style? We may initially think of the way people dress, their hairstyle, or even the vehicle they drive. But a crucial part of a person's style is the way they speak. How we talk can tell other people a lot about our self or who we would like to be. It can be a strong indication of where we are from, our level of education and our age, and it can also reveal a lot about how we view the situation in which we are speaking. Because we are largely unaware of our language production and language behaviour, we are often not conscious of features in our language that give away which social groups we belong to or even which values we hold. On the other hand, we may be very aware of the linguistic features that are characteristic of another social group, and we may consciously choose to adopt those language features to indicate that we are part of that group – or would like to be, at least. One thing is clear: an individual can change their linguistic style just as easily as they can change their fashion style or hairstyle, if not more easily. This ability to change language style is called style shifting and it happens all the time.

B Style shifting is not an addition to how we normally speak; in fact, you could say that it is impossible to speak without any style. When we speak, we are making several choices within fractions of a second; choices regarding vocabulary, pronunciation, intonation, grammar, sentence length and dialect. Mostly these choices are unconscious and have been learnt in childhood. The most noticeable of the language features that we learn unconsciously are determined by the place where we grow up and may include the vocabulary and grammar patterns of the dialect spoken in that area.

C Other choices are conscious and may be tied to our work; newsreaders or teachers, for example, may speak in a certain way due to their jobs. Personal language style is therefore an individual version of the typical behaviour of a social group and is acquired along with the culture of the group. Moreover, as we grow up and come into contact with other social groups, we continually adjust our speech to the audience, situation and topic.

D So, style shifting is the change we make, consciously or unconsciously, to our personal language depending on the circumstances. And how do we shift our linguistic style? The most common moves are from casual to formal or vice versa. Casual to formal shifts happen in specific contexts and in certain social groups. They are marked by a reduction in certain features of casual speech, such as the use of double negatives or slang words. They are also marked by hypercorrection. Hypercorrection is the over-use of a perceived rule from a more 'prestigious' variety of the language. An example from English is as follows: instead of saying 'There's no difference between you and me', a style shift to more formal speech would be 'There's no difference between you and I'. Conversely, a shift from formal to informal will be marked by greater use of informal speech features. Another type of style shift occurs when we change our style in response to our audience. An example is when an adult speaks to a baby in 'baby language', or again, when a newsreader stops using their personal speech style and begins to use their 'newsreader' style.

E   There are a number of theories for why people change their personal speech style. The first was put forward by William Labov in the 1960s. Labov studied the speech patterns of people in New York, and in particular the pronunciation of /r/ – the inclusion of this sound being seen as high status. Labov found that because people were aware of the higher status of this sound, when they were asked to do a task that needed their attention such as reading aloud, they were more likely to produce the sound. On the other hand, when asked to do something which involved their emotions, like telling a story, they paid less attention to the sound. This is called the Attention to Speech model. Another theory, the Communication Accommodation Theory, developed by Howard Giles in the 1970s, says that style shift may be convergent, i.e. it moves closer to the speech style of the person or people with whom we are talking, or it may be divergent, i.e. it moves away from the other person's speech style. The shift is most commonly convergent when people find similarities in their background, social class or even shared interests and likes. In a later theory, the role of the other speaker or audience is emphasised further. In 1984 Allan Bell proposed the Audience Design Model. In this theory, individuals shift their style to win the approval of the people they are speaking to.

F   Whatever reason is closest to the truth, whether we pay more attention to how we say something, express social solidarity or seek the approval of our audience, it is clear that everyone possesses the ability to change their language identity according to who they are speaking to and how they would like to project themselves.

Questions 14–19

Do the following statements agree with the information given in Reading Passage 2?
Write

TRUE	*if the statement agrees with the information*
FALSE	*if the statement contradicts the information*
NOT GIVEN	*if there is no information on this*

14   We are usually aware of the way we use language in our speech.

15   If we wanted to, we could speak in a neutral style.

16   Our language choices happen virtually instantaneously.

17   Some people use certain styles of speech as part of their job.

18   Informal to formal style shifting features a greater use of personal pronouns.

19   Labov's experiments included asking people to read a text out loud.

Questions 20–25

Classify the following as part of

    A *Attention Theory*

    B *Communication Accommodation Theory*

    C *Audience Design Model*

*Write the correct letter, **A**, **B** or **C**, next to Questions 20–25.*

20 reading aloud

21 showing you are similar to someone by shifting your speech style to theirs

22 narrating

23 trying to gain your listener's acceptance

24 including a particular sound

25 moving your speech style away from the other person's

Question 26

26 Which of the following is NOT an example of style shift?

    A being unaware of your speech style

    B changing pronunciation features

    C using unusual sentence patterns

    D using dialect words in your speech

READING PASSAGE 3

*You should spend about 20 minutes on **Questions 27–40**, which are based on Reading Passage 3 below.*

Coronal Mass Ejections

Quebec, 13th March 1989: At 2.45 a.m. the province's entire power grid crashed. The blackout affected six million people in north-eastern Canada for up to nine hours, shutting schools and businesses, and closing down the Montreal Metro and Dorval Airport. Meanwhile, a red glow appeared in the night sky over most of the world, and as far south as Texas and Cuba people were able to see multi-coloured shifting lights in the sky. At the same time, in space, some satellites spun out of control for several hours. The blackout in Quebec was caused when the safety systems in the electricity network sensed a power surge caused by electric energy flowing through the ground. In fact, most of North America was experiencing increased electrical activity and around 200 power grid problems were reported within minutes of each other.

All the events had one source: days earlier a massive wave of energy had erupted from the sun and crashed into earth's magnetic field. These events are called coronal mass ejections (CMEs). CMEs are similar to solar flares in so far as they both produce high-energy particles that are dangerous to living organisms. They are both explosions on the surface of the sun that continue for minutes and even hours, and they can release enough energy to power the USA for a million years. They happen when areas of intense solar activity called sunspots appear and magnetic fields associated with sunspots connect, sending huge amounts of energy away from the sun. The most dangerous emissions from these ejections are protons (subatomic particles with a positive electrical charge) and X-rays.

The sun has an eleven-year cycle of activity in which the intensity of activity on its surface changes, the most intense period (called a solar maximum) being characterised by the appearance of sun spots and solar flares. Like solar flares, CMEs are more likely to be produced during the period of maximum solar activity. However, unlike solar flares, which produce high-energy particles near the surface of the sun, CMEs carry a large volume of material much further into interplanetary space. Fortunately, the iron core spinning at the centre of the Earth generates a magnetic force field around the planet called the magnetosphere. This magnetic field reaches out thousands of miles into space and protects us from all but the most violent CMEs. When the solar material collides with the earth's magnetosphere, it triggers geomagnetic storms of the kind that affected Quebec so dramatically.

CMEs and flares are classified as B, C, M or X according to how strong they are. Each letter of the scale is ten times more powerful than the previous one; so an X flare is ten times more powerful than an M and a hundred times more powerful than a C flare. Within each letter scale there is a finer gradation from 1 to 9. In reality, C class flares are too weak to affect the Earth; M class flares can cause radio blackouts in areas near the poles and cause weak radiation storms that can be dangerous for astronauts. However, the X class flares can cause considerable damage at ground level. Although the flare that affected Quebec was strong, the most powerful flare ever recorded was in 2003 – a flare so powerful that it overloaded satellite sensors.

It will typically take a CME three to five days to affect the Earth after leaving the sun. Observing the ejection of CMEs from the sun provides early warning of geomagnetic storms. The Solar and Heliospheric Observatory, a European-built spacecraft that orbits the Earth, continuously observes the CMEs to determine if they are travelling in the direction of the Earth as damage to satellites and communications can be very serious. Communications satellites are generally the most exposed to damage from CMEs – these satellites are often in high orbits. When the solar material hits a satellite, it becomes charged with electricity and a component can become damaged by the current or by high-energy particles penetrating the satellite. As we have become more and more dependent upon high technology and other systems that can be affected by electrical currents and energy particles, the danger from flares and CMEs has intensified. But could a solar flare or CME be large enough to cause a global disaster? It is impossible to give an answer.

Questions 27–30

Choose the correct letter, A, B or C.

27 What did the CME of 13th March 1989 NOT do?

   A disrupt daily life for some Canadians

   B cause an unusual phenomenon in Texas

   C stop all flights across Canada

   D increase ground electricity in North America

28 What produces the magnetosphere?

   A high-energy particles

   B geomagnetic storms

   C metal at the centre of the Earth

   D sunspots

29 What does the Solar and Heliospheric Observatory do?

   A It tells scientists when a CME is approaching the Earth.

   B It communicates with other satellites orbiting the Earth.

   C It tells scientists if a CME will cause a global disaster.

   D It circles the sun in a high orbit.

30 How can CMEs damage satellites?

   A by sending them out of high orbit

   B by bombarding them with high-energy particles

   C by stopping communication between them and the sun

   D by melting components inside them

Questions 31–35

Which characterises the following?

    A solar flare

    B CME

    C both

*Write the correct letter, **A**, **B** or **C**, next to Questions 31–35.*

31 It is produced during the solar maximum.

32 It carries material far into interplanetary space.

33 It produces high-energy particles.

34 It may affect the Earth.

35 It happens near the sun's surface.

Questions 36–40

Which flares are mentioned in the text as having the effects below?

    A C flares

    B M flares

    C X flares

*Write the correct letter, **A**, **B**, or **C**, next to Questions 36–40.*

36 There would be damage to electrical equipment on the Earth's surface.

37 You couldn't listen to the radio in certain places.

38 You wouldn't notice the effect.

39 You would be harmed if you were working in space.

40 It would seriously damage satellite equipment.

WRITING TASK 1

You should spend about 20 minutes on this task.

The graph below shows the reasons for the use of social media by businesses, by size of business, in 2012.

Summarise the information by selecting and reporting the main features, and make comparisons where relevant.

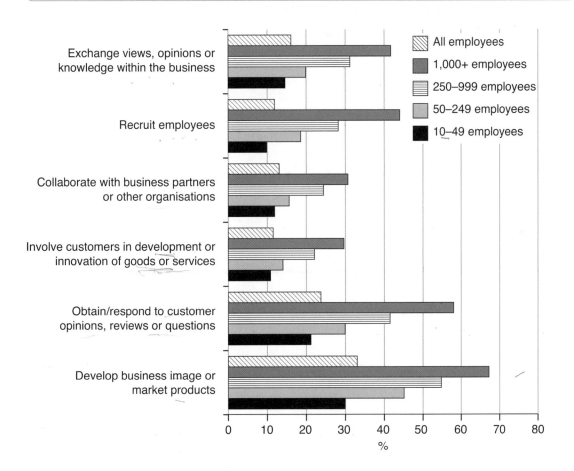

Write at least 150 words.

WRITING TASK 2

You should spend about 40 minutes on this task.

Write about the following topic:

> Young people are often the first to suffer when job opportunities are scarce.
>
> In which ways does age affect employment opportunities?
>
> How might employers deal with the issue fairly?

Give reasons for your answer and include any relevant examples from your own knowledge or experience.

Write at least 250 words.

SPEAKING

PART 1: Introduction and interview

Listen to Track 12, pressing pause after each question to answer.

🎧 12

PART 2: Individual long turn

Before you read the task card, listen to Track 13.

🎧 13

Describe an important letter or email you once received.

You should say
> when you received it
> who sent it to you
> what the letter/email was about
and say why it was so important to you.

PART 3: Two-way discussion

Listen to Track 14, pressing pause after each question to answer.

🎧 14

company.

Test 3

SECTION 1   Questions 1–10

15

Questions 1–3

Choose the correct letter, A, B or C.

> *Example*
> What has the patient just had?
> **A** a tooth out
> **B** his teeth cleaned
> **C** (an X-ray)

1 On which day can the patient make an appointment?

   A Monday

   B Tuesday

   C Wednesday

2 The patient has to wait for an appointment because

   A the surgery is closed for a holiday.

   B there are fewer dentists available.

   C a dentist has cancelled some appointments.

3 The patient books an appointment at

   A 1.30.

   B 3.30.

   C 4.00.

Questions 4–6

Complete the notes below.

*Write **NO MORE THAN TWO WORDS** or **A NUMBER** for each answer.*

Costs of treatment

Fillings   £55

Extractions   £90

X-rays   **(4)** £ _____

We require **(5)** _____ hours notice of a cancellation, otherwise a fee of £10 is charged.

Cheques should be made payable to **(6)** _____ Dental Surgeons.

Questions 7–10

Complete the notes below.

*Write **NO MORE THAN TWO WORDS** for each answer.*

Dental Insurance

We cover up to £650 worth of treatment every **(7)** _____.

Get big discounts on insurance cover for the whole **(8)** _____.

You can pay **(9)** _____ and no interest is charged.

Cover begins immediately your **(10)** _____ starts.

🎧
16

Question 11

Choose the correct letter, A, B or C.

The main aim of the arts festival is to

    A support the creative industries.

    B increase the number of spectators.

    C get more people into the creative arts.

Questions 12–13

Choose TWO letters, A–E.

Which **TWO** things does the speaker say about doing something creative?

    A It is best to attend a workshop.

    B It can remind you of your childhood.

    C It can give joy to other people.

    D You may be surprised how talented you are.

    E You can become more interested in the world around you.

Questions 14–17

Which groups of people can do the following activities?

Write the letters A, B, C or D next to Questions 14–17.

> **A** older people
>
> **B** any interested people
>
> **C** the unemployed
>
> **D** creative people

Activities

14 Create your own Artwork

15 Walk for Creativity

16 Work with Children

17 Learn the Art of Story-telling

Questions 18–20

Complete the sentences below.

*Write **NO MORE THAN TWO WORDS OR A NUMBER** for each answer.*

Sessions must be **(18)** _____ in advance.

All workshops are free of charge and **(19)** _____ will be provided.

The office is open from 9–5, Monday–Friday, and until **(20)** _____ on Saturdays.

Questions 21–23

What does Judy say about the following courses?

*Write the correct letter, **A**, **B** or **C** next to Questions 21–23.*

    A She transferred from this course.

    B She transferred to this course.

    C Her transfer request was turned down for this course.

21 Fine Art

22 History of Art

23 English

Questions 24–26

*Choose **THREE** letters, **A–G**.*

Which **THREE** reasons does Graham give for wanting to transfer?

    A The German course is too difficult.

    B He does not like the people he is studying with.

    C He has more interest in history.

    D He plans to do a combined degree.

    E It suits his career plans.

    F He is not bothered that he will not spend a year abroad.

    G His housemate has persuaded him to transfer.

Questions 27–30

Complete the sentences below.

*Write **NO MORE THAN THREE WORDS** for each answer.*

Transferring to another course at the university

Step 1: Identify your reasons for wanting to transfer.

Step 2: Check that you satisfy the **(27)** _____ for the new course.

Step 3: Speak with the Careers Service.

Step 4: Find out if there are any **(28)** _____ implications.

Step 5: Speak to the Admissions Tutor in the department you want to transfer to.

Step 6: Complete a(n) **(29)** _____ form.

Please note: The form must also be signed by the **(30)** _____ of your current course and the one you are transferring to.

Questions 31–40

Choose the correct letter, A, B or C.

31 The symptoms of synaesthesia

    A are the same for everyone with the condition.

    B cannot be controlled.

    C can be harmful.

32 People who discover that they have synaesthesia

    A often say they thought everyone experienced it.

    B express negative feelings about their condition.

    C wonder what it is like to be normal.

33 One research project looking at synaesthesia

    A produced different results from other research.

    B was able to estimate the proportion of people with the condition.

    C found that a small number of people saw different colours.

34 The condition means some people see numbers or letters

    A as either red or blue.

    B as days or months.

    C as colours or in particular relative positions.

35 The way people experience colours

    A will be exactly the same for everyone.

    B can lead to disagreements.

    C differs when a large number of experiments are carried out.

36 When seeing certain words, people with word–taste synaesthesia

   A will differ in the way they 'taste' a word.

   B generally get a sweet taste in their mouth.

   C have similar experiences.

37 What does the speaker say about synaesthesia?

   A Infants may all have the condition.

   B It is difficult to prove that the condition exists.

   C The condition becomes more noticeable during childhood.

38 Family members with synaesthesia

   A are not always closely related.

   B may not have the same symptoms.

   C make up forty per cent of the extended family.

39 People with synaesthesia

   A are advised to take up a hobby or interest.

   B are often talented artists.

   C often take an interest in the arts.

40 What attitude do scientists have towards synaesthesia nowadays?

   A It has little scientific worth.

   B It may help them better understand how the brain functions.

   C They need more proof that it exists.

READING PASSAGE 1

*You should spend about 20 minutes on **Questions 1–12**, which are based on Reading Passage 1 below.*

A A condition that causes children to dislike being hugged and sometimes reject all physical affection is closer to being understood following research into the part of the brain responsible for our senses. Scientists at Northwestern University, Illinois, and the University of Edinburgh explored fragile X syndrome, a condition associated with hypersensitivity to sounds, touch, smells and visual stimuli that can result in social withdrawal or anxiety. Hypersensitivity is a condition in which the person affected responds in an excessive way to contact with the world around them. Some sufferers are even hypersensitive to material on their skin.

B The scientists found that critical phases in the brain's development may be wrongly timed in people with the condition. This may result in delayed communication between certain neurons in the brain. By recording electrical signals in the brains of mice, bred to exactly copy the effects of the condition, the researchers found that connections in the brain's sensory cortex were late to develop fully. The study, published in the journal *Neuron*, found that normal neural connections in the sensory cortex occur much earlier than previously thought: in the first week of pregnancy in mice, which is equivalent to the middle of the second trimester (or fifth month) of pregnancy in humans. In fragile X syndrome, the mistiming also has a domino effect, causing further problems with the correct wiring of the brain. The hope is that by understanding how and when the functions of the brain are affected in fragile X syndrome, a therapy may become possible.

C 'There is a "critical period" during development, when the brain is very plastic and is changing rapidly,' said Anis Contractor, from the Feinberg School of Medicine at Northwestern University. 'All the elements of this rapid development have to be coordinated so that the brain becomes wired correctly and therefore functions properly.' People with the syndrome have cognitive problems as well as sensory problems that make them physically weaker. 'They have tactile defensiveness,' Dr Contractor said. 'They don't look in people's eyes, they won't hug their parents, and they are hypersensitive to touch and sound. All of this causes anxiety for family and friends as well as for the fragile X patients themselves.' Peter Kind, who led the study at the University of Edinburgh, said: 'We know there are key windows during which the brain develops, both in the womb and afterwards. The general principle is that if these time windows have shifted, then that could explain the cognitive problems.'

D Professor Kind said that this could be demonstrated by the fact that a child with a cataract (a medical condition in which the lens of the eye becomes less and less transparent) that was not corrected would become permanently blind in the affected eye, whereas an adult would be able to regain their sight after an operation. 'We've learnt that these changes happen much earlier than previously thought, which gives valuable insight into when we should begin therapeutic intervention for people with these conditions,' he said. 'It also has implications for the treatment of autism since the changes in the brains of people with fragile X syndrome and autistic people are thought to significantly overlap.' Autism, as many people know, is a disability that affects how a person communicates with and relates to other people, and how they make sense of the world.

E Fragile X syndrome is as common as cystic fibrosis, a genetic disorder that commonly affects the lungs and causes breathing difficulties, and that affects about 1 in 4,000 males and 1 in 8,000 females worldwide. The Fragile X Society believes that there are many people who have the fragile X syndrome but have never been diagnosed. It shows up in early infancy and progressively worsens throughout childhood, causing intellectual disability as well as social, language and behavioural problems.

F Fragile X syndrome is caused by a gene mutation on the X chromosome – one of the two chromosomes that determine the gender or sex of a person. The mutation interferes in the production of a protein called fragile X mental retardation protein. Fragile X is so-named because the X chromosome appears broken or kinked. Tim Potter, of the Fragile X Society, said: 'We welcome any research that helps us understand fragile X and which may open the way to reversing the effects or preventing them ever happening.'

Questions 1–5

Reading Passage 1 has six paragraphs, A–F.

Choose the correct heading for paragraphs A, B, C, D and F from the list of headings below.

Write the correct number, i–ix, next to Questions 1–5.

List of Headings

i	How fragile X syndrome was discovered
ii	The genetic basis of fragile X syndrome
iii	Fragile X syndrome and developmental delays in the brain
iv	New treatments for fragile X syndrome
v	The comparative frequency of fragile X syndrome
vi	Research into understanding fragile X syndrome
vii	Reasons for the increase of fragile X syndrome
viii	Other conditions related to cognitive development
ix	Examples of the symptoms of Fragile X syndrome

Example	Answer
Paragraph **E**	v

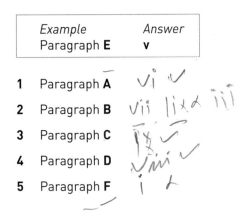

1   Paragraph **A**   vi
2   Paragraph **B**   vii lixd iii
3   Paragraph **C**   ix
4   Paragraph **D**   viii
5   Paragraph **F**   i

Questions 6–10

Complete the summary of paragraphs A and B below.

Choose NO MORE THAN TWO WORDS from the passage for each answer.

Write your answers in spaces 6–11.

People with fragile X syndrome are extremely sensitive to sensory **(6)** _____cortex_____ ~~stimuli condition~~.
Some sufferers are even **(7)** _____hypersensitive_____ to clothing. The condition is the
result of connections within the **(8)** _____sensory cortex_____ of the brain not being made ~~neuron~~
at the right time. Instead, the **(9)** _____neuron_____ of people with the condition
establish connections later than should happen, which is normally in the second
(10) _____trimester_____ of pregnancy in humans. By understanding how the brain's
(11) _____mistiming_____ / _wiring_ are affected, scientists hope to develop a treatment.

Question 12

Complete the title of Reading Passage 3.

Choose the correct letter, A, B, C or D.

Study reveals common bond of children who

    (A) are autistic.

    (B) hate to be hugged. ◌

    C have incomplete X chromosomes.

*You should spend about 20 minutes on **Questions 13–26**, which are based on Reading Passage 2 below.*

Mutualism

Mutualism is an association between individuals belonging to two different species that benefit each other. There are numerous examples of this: the way flowers rely on insects to pollinate them or even how we humans rely on bacteria within our digestive system to break down our food.

One of the most visible forms of mutualism can be found in the pampas grasslands of Argentina, where organisms belonging to two different species work together not only to benefit each other but also to change the ecosystem around them. Grasscutter ants have been instrumental in shaping the landscape of the pampas grasslands – in fact, the landscape has been created almost entirely by the ants. Although they are only 1.5 cm long, they are one of the few creatures capable of shaping their own environment and one of the few living creatures apart from humans that cultivate their own food. The ants harvest the grasslands to supply their colony with grass. Each year over 0.5 tonnes of grass are harvested by a single colony. However, grass consists largely of cellulose, which the ants cannot digest, so the ants have developed a mutualistic relationship with an organism that can digest it. Deep inside the ant nests is a fungus that is able to grow on the compost produced by the grass. The fungus is unique to the habitat inside the ants' nest and it produces edible gardens for the ants. The relationship is so successful that a single colony can consist of up to eight million ants.

One of the reasons for the ants' success is the sophistication of their social organisation: they are all members of a single society but there is a division of labour within it. There are three main castes: the queen, the soldiers (or majors) and the worker ants. The worker ants are further divided into categories: the minims (the smallest ants), the minors and the mediae, each with different duties. The soldier ants defend the colony against physical threats. They also clear the paths for the other workers. The mediae are the foraging ants that look for grass to cut up and take back to the nest. Once the grass has been harvested, the forager ants carry it to the nest by following a chemical trail. But often they are not alone: minims ride on them or on the grass in order to protect them from a particular species of fly that parasitises the foragers. As soon as the grass leaves arrive at the nest, the forager ants pass them to smaller gardener ants, which cut up the leaves into smaller and smaller pieces until they are small enough to feed to the fungus. They then pass the tiny pieces on to the smallest ants, which feed the grass to the fungus and tend the fungal gardens.

A very important function of the smallest ants is to keep the fungus healthy. They do this by carefully inspecting each piece of grass leaf and making sure that it is free from other fungi or pests. In fact, the mutualistic relationship is supplemented by bacteria that live on the ants and give out chemicals that kill microbes harmful to the fungus. The relationship between the fungus and the ants is so developed that the grasscutter ants are sensitive to the fungus's reaction to different plants; if a particular plant is poisonous to the fungus, the ants no longer collect it. Waste disposal is another serious concern. Waste is collected by waste-disposer ants, which tend to be the older ants, thus ensuring that the younger ones can tend to other work. The waste-disposer ants remove waste (including dead ants) from the nest and take it underground into the deepest tunnels, where they aid its decomposition by moving it around.

Because the fungus at the heart of the colony nest is a living and breathing organism, it produces carbon dioxide – a very toxic gas. The ant nest is a masterpiece of construction, carefully made to keep air circulating in order to prevent suffocation through the build-up of carbon dioxide. The nest has two methods of air circulation. Firstly, the hot air produced by the fungal gardens at the centre of the nest flows up through a central tunnel and draws in cooler, cleaner air from the outside passages. The second method involves a series of towers at the top of the nest. When the wind blows over the towers, it draws out old air and fresh air rushes into the nest from nest holes that extend outwards from the main nest. A nest can measure up to 30 metres across, and other mounds extend away from the central nest for up to 80 metres. As the nest also dominates the underground world, often extending seven metres down, the rapid flow of air through the nest is essential to the health of the inhabitants and their garden.

Questions 13–19

Do the following statements agree with the information given in Reading Passage 2?
Write

TRUE	*if the statement agrees with the information*
FALSE	*if the statement contradicts the information*
NOT GIVEN	*if there is no information on this*

13 Grasscutter ants are one of a small group of creatures that use other organisms to produce food.

14 The fungus that grows in the nests of grasscutter ants is not found in any other kind of environment.

15 Grasscutter ants cut the grass into very small pieces so they can eat it.

16 Forager ants are the smallest ants.

17 Grasscutter ants can carry loads much heavier than their body weight.

18 The ants never collect plants that might harm the fungus.

19 The older ants are responsible for getting rid of waste.

Questions 20–23

Classify the following as typical of

    A majors

    B mediae

    C minims

Write the correct letter, A, B or C, next to Questions 20–23.

20 take grass back to the colony

21 protect the colony from invaders

22 make sure the way to the food is clear

23 farm the fungus

Questions 24–26

Label the diagram below using words from the box.

Write the correct letter, A–C, in spaces 24–26.

A	fungal gardens
B	waste tunnel
C	carbon dioxide

24 ~~A~~ C

wind

fungs B. A 25

fresh air

B 26

READING PASSAGE 3

*You should spend about 20 minutes on **Questions 27–40**, which are based on Reading Passage 3 below.*

Is it really true that human adults are less able to learn as they grow older? Traditionally, the brain was thought to be 'completed' at the latest by the start of adulthood. During adulthood the brain was viewed as relatively stable until at last the aging brain started to decline. We have around 86 billion neurons at birth, and that's it. Or is it? Until two decades ago, it was thought that new neurons – the cells that carry messages between the brain and other parts of the body – did not grow in adults. Moreover, it was believed that functions in the brain were fixed or localised in distinct areas, one common assumption being that language functions resided solely in the left hemisphere of the brain. The functions were fixed in childhood and did not change.

But this is not strictly true. Research has shown that adult brains are not fixed, and nor are they degenerating or dying as we grow older. In fact, the opposite seems to be the case: neurons are dying and being regenerated all the time and new experiences create new connections between neurons. Furthermore, when the brain suffers damage, it has the ability to shift brain functions to other parts of the brain.

The first evidence that refuted the idea that the brain was a stable organ was produced over 30 years ago. Fernando Nottebohm's study of male songbirds at The Rockerfeller University showed that new neurons would grow when a bird learnt a new song. And more recently, evidence from studies done at Wayne State University has shown that physical exercise or lack of it is a factor in remodelling the brain. Two regions of the brain are capable of producing new neurons: the hippocampus and the olfactory cortex. In particular, the hippocampus is extremely important in turning short-term memories into long-term memories. It appears that new neurons regularly grow and move into the hippocampus. Conversely, the loss of brain tissue, most often associated with brain damage or illness can also have a positive function. We know that most of the neurons that die off in children and adults are the ones that are not effective or are not needed. In short, the brain needs to operate at maximum efficiency and neurons which become unused are discarded. So, far from being a stable organ, the brain is constantly changing, losing what is not needed and developing what is needed.

A landmark study by neuroscientist Dr Eleanor Maguire and her colleagues at University College, London confirmed findings from other studies which reveal that when humans spend time repeating a particular skill, the area of the brain associated with that skill becomes better developed. For four years, Dr Maguire and her team followed a group of 79 London taxi drivers who shared certain characteristics including age, gender and education. They used magnetic resonance imaging (MRI) to map changes to their posterior hippocampi. The hippocampus plays a major role in short-term memory and spatial navigation, both of which are very important to the work of taxi drivers, and London taxi drivers in particular. To become a taxi driver in London, you need to learn 'the Knowledge' – a detailed understanding of the streets in central London as well as tourist spots and other places of interest. Gaining 'the Knowledge' takes on average three to four years, at the end of which taxi drivers have to take a test that only fifty per cent of candidates pass.

At the start of the study, the taxi drivers had similar sized hippocampi but after four years of intensive spatial and memory training, Dr Maguire found that the taxi drivers who successfully passed their tests had more developed hippocampi than those who failed. This was confirmed by a series of memory tests and MRI images which showed that certain parts of their brains had developed over time. Furthermore, other experimental studies over the last few decades have shown that the adult brain can change its structure and function massively. In a 1982 study carried out by Jon Kaas at Vanderbilt University, changes in brain patterns were noted in people whose limbs had been amputated or who suffered nerve damage. Since then, it has become clear that the living brain is constantly changing depending on external experiences. As Boston University neurobiologist Howard Eichenbaum (commenting on Dr Maguire's research) stated: '... you can produce profound changes in the brain with training. That's a big deal.'

Questions 27–32

Complete the sentences below.

*Choose **NO MORE THAN THREE WORDS** or a **NUMBER** from the passage for each answer.*

Write your answers in spaces 27–32.

27 Humans are born with about _____ neurons.

28 It used to be believed that neurons _____ in humans after a certain age.

29 If the brain is damaged, it can _____ to other areas within the brain.

30 The hippocampus, which plays a role in creating _____ from short-term memories, has been identified as being one of the parts of the brain that can grow neurons.

31 The hippocampus also plays an important part in _____ a key skill for taxi drivers in London.

32 Taxi drivers who successfully passed 'the Knowledge' had _____ hippocampi than those who did not pass.

Questions 33–36

Look at the people and institutions (Questions 33–36) and the list of findings below.

Match each person or institution with their findings.

Write the correct letter, *A–G*, next to Questions 33–36. Note: There are three more findings than you will need.

Findings

    A The hippocampus stores memories.

    B Song birds grew neurons when they learnt a new song.

    C The olfactory cortex is capable of growing new cells.

    D Being active changes the brain.

    E The brain is constantly changing its function and structure.

    F Training for a test enlarged a part of the brain in some people.

    G Brain patterns changed when a person's arms or legs were cut off.

33 Fernando Nottebohm, The Rockefeller University   B

34 Jon Kaas, Vanderbilt University   G

35 Eleanor Maguire, University College, London   A

36 Wayne State University   D

Questions 37–40

Do the following statements agree with the information given in Reading Passage 3?

Write

    TRUE   *if the statement agrees with the information*
    FALSE   *if the statement contradicts the information*
    NOT GIVEN *if there is no information on this*

37 When you do something over and over again, the part of the brain controlling the skill grows. T

38 'The Knowledge' helps taxi drivers to take people to places in the shortest time. NG

39 Dr Maguire's study was conducted on people with similar characteristics.

40 Dr Maguire relied mainly on intelligence tests in her research. F

WRITING

WRITING TASK 1

You should spend about 20 minutes on this task.

> The graph below shows the spending of UK residents on visits abroad between 1993 and 2013.
>
> Summarise the information by selecting and reporting the main features, and make comparisons where relevant.

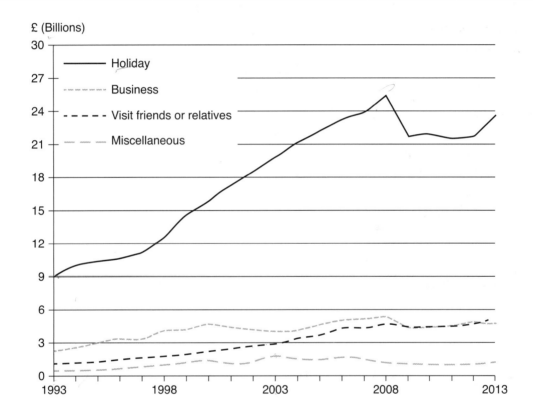

Write at least 150 words.

WRITING TASK 2

You should spend about 40 minutes on this task.

Write about the following topic:

> *Hosting a major sporting event such as the Olympics or the football World Cup offers significant benefits to the country concerned, yet the costs involved can be excessive and may divert funds from other important areas.*
>
> *What are the benefits of being a host, and do these outweigh the financial implications?*

Give reasons for your answer and include any relevant examples from your own knowledge or experience.

Write at least 250 words.

SPEAKING

PART 1: Introduction and interview

Listen to Track 19, pressing pause after each question to answer.

PART 2: Individual long turn

Before you read the task card, listen to Track 20.

Describe a favourite item of clothing you own.

You should say

what the item is

how long you have had it

when you tend to wear it

and say what it is about this item of clothing that makes it special.

PART 3: Two-way discussion

Listen to Track 21, pressing pause after each question to answer.

Test 4

SECTION 1   Questions 1–10

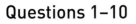

Questions 1–10

Complete the notes below.

*Write **NO MORE THAN THREE WORDS** or **A NUMBER** for each answer.*

> *Example*
> The woman was getting something *for lunch* when the accident happened.

Accident report

Time of accident: **(1)** _____

Driver failed to stop at the junction of Monks Road and High Street.

There were **(2)** _____ people in the car, all around 20 years old.

The car hit a woman on her **(3)** _____.

The car was last seen heading towards the **(4)** _____.

The **(5)** _____ at the junction are out of order.

The car may have been a red Ford Fiesta. One of the car doors is **(6)** _____.

Registration number: Y48 **(7)** _____

Witness name: Rita **(8)** _____

Address: 19, **(9)** _____

Telephone number: 0232 566788

Mobile number: **(10)** 07834 _____

23

SECTION 2   *Questions 11–20*

Questions 11–12

Choose the correct letter, A, B or C.

11 The speaker says solar panels

    A are expensive.

    B should be considered more seriously.

    C are not very popular.

12 In the speaker's opinion, most people

    A neglect to turn the heating down.

    B wash their clothes too often.

    C do not use the kitchen efficiently.

Questions 13–20

Complete the notes below.

*Write **NO MORE THAN THREE WORDS** or **A NUMBER** for each answer.*

Energy-saving tips

Living in **(13)** _____ accommodation? Check windows and doors for draughts.

Don't leave laptops and TVs on **(14)** _____ overnight.

Don't use **(15)** _____ than you need when making hot drinks.

Put **(16)** _____ pots and pans when boiling water.

Where possible, avoid placing the refrigerator next to the **(17)** _____ .

Remember to turn down the fridge temperature control in the **(18)** _____ .

Don't forget to **(19)** _____ the freezer and don't put too much food in it.

Reduce the temperature of your washing machine to **(20)** _____ degrees.

Questions 21–25

Choose the correct letter, A, B or C.

21 What did Alice do when she first arrived at the university Open Day?

    A She had a coffee.

    B She looked around the campus.

    C She went to one of the events.

22 Which of the following is NOT on the campus?

    A a supermarket

    B a bank

    C a bookshop

23 Why does Oliver think it is a good idea to register?

    A The university will know you attended.

    B You get an information pack.

    C You cannot attend events unless you register.

24 What is the main factor for Alice in her choice of university?

    A its facilities

    B its links to industry

    C the number of mature students

25 Which area of work is Oliver interested in?

    A teaching

    B finance

    C software development

Questions 26–28

What does Alice say about the events in the afternoon?

Write the correct letter, A, B or C next to Questions 26–28.

    A She will attend.

    B She might attend.

    C She will not attend.

26 a talk about the year abroad

27 the exhibition in the Physics Department

28 a talk by the head of department

Questions 29–30

Choose the correct letter, A, B or C.

29 Which employers offer only unpaid work?

    A accountancy firms

    B the university

    C campus retail outlets

30 Oliver

    A plans to live at home if he gets a place at the university.

    B will live on campus if he gets a place at the university.

    C does not yet know where he will live if he gets a place at the university.

Questions 31–40

Complete the lecture notes below.

*Write **NO MORE THAN TWO WORDS** for each answer.*

Pygmy Blue Whale Research

- Pygmy blue whales: Before 1966 it is likely they were **(31)** _____ with the Antarctic blue whales.

- Aim of study: To find out more about their **(32)** _____ and movements.

- Method: Whales are tagged with an antenna. When the antenna communicates with a number of satellites, the whale's **(33)** _____ can be identified. Researchers access the results using the project **(34)** _____.

- Findings: The whales travel from the **(35)** _____ of Australia to breeding grounds in Indonesia during March and April, and return to Australian waters in **(36)** _____. Pygmy whales do not go without **(37)** _____ whilst they are in their breeding grounds.

- Conservation issues: The effect of **(38)** _____ routes on communication between whales.
  Conservation efforts can take place over a(n) **(39)** _____ area now there is evidence that they migrate out of Australian waters.

- Future studies: To explore whether pygmy whales off the southern coast of Australia follow the same northerly migratory routes as those studied or whether they travel to a(n) **(40)** _____ region to the south of Australia.

READING

READING PASSAGE 1

*You should spend about 20 minutes on **Questions 1–13**, which are based on Reading Passage 1 below.*

Meteor Strikes

On 15 February 2013, just after dawn, the sleepy Russian city of Chelyabinsk was woken by the biggest meteor strike on Earth in over 100 years. Several people videoed the meteor as it crashed through Earth's atmosphere, passing close above the city and giving scientists vital clues as to where it had come from and how it had travelled to Earth. To the people of Chelyabinsk, the meteor shone 30 times brighter than the sun and had 20–30 times more energy than the atomic bomb dropped on Hiroshima. The meteor did not hit the ground, but due to its enormous speed exploded 29.7 kilometres above the ground, producing a bright flash, a cloud of hot dust and gas, many smaller fragments of meteor and a powerful shockwave. The latter was so strong that it knocked people off their feet and blew out the windows of homes, shops and factories. 1,500 people went to hospital with injuries indirectly caused by the strike, but matters could have been far worse if the meteor had made contact with the Earth.

The meteor was not an uncommon rock. From studying videos of the meteor's flight, scientists have concluded that it originated in the asteroid belt located between the orbits of Mars and Jupiter. At the time it entered Earth's atmosphere, it weighed between 12,000 and 13,000 metric tonnes and was 10 metres in diameter. It crashed through the upper atmosphere at around 19 kilometres a second – above 50 times the speed of sound, fracturing at an altitude of between 45 and 50 kilometres. Such events happen on average every 10 or so years, mainly over oceans or unpopulated areas. This time the strike was over a city and observed by many people, reminding us how common these occurrences are.

A meteor strike has several phases. Moving through space, a meteor's temperature can be around −100°C. It travels around 5 kilometres per second until Earth's gravity accelerates it to 17 kilometres a second. It begins to encounter the atmosphere 140 kilometres above the Earth but there is little air resistance until about three seconds later, when it reaches 100 kilometres above the ground. At this point the air becomes dense, causing the meteor to glow as the material on its surface melts. The mix of burning gas and dust creates a fireball as the meteor loses 3 to 6 millimetres of surface mass per second as it is heated to over 1,800°C. The rate of loss of material through heat is so rapid that the core temperature of the meteor is still very low while at the same time a tail of vaporised dust and gas becomes visible. These tails can often be seen for up to 45 minutes and may be followed by a sonic boom as the meteor crashes through the sound barrier. During its flight to the Earth, the meteor slows down by 70 per cent and it is during this period that it may fracture and split. At this point some meteors explode in a violent airburst while others enter dark flight – the period when the meteor slows down so much that it stops burning and it falls to the ground as a cold rock.

The Chelyabinsk airburst left only a few large pieces of the meteor: one rock was recovered near the town of Timiryazevskiy, another fell on a house in Deputatskiy, and the largest piece was found by divers at the bottom of Lake Chebarkul. The meteor was the largest to crash to Earth since 1908, when a meteor exploded over an area near the Tunguska River in Siberia. Although information about the event is scarce, the theory most scientists share is that an asteroid around 36.5 metres in diameter and travelling at 54,000 kilometres per hour entered the atmosphere above Russia. It exploded in an airburst at 28,000 feet, releasing energy equal to about 185 Hiroshima atomic bombs and flattening trees across an area of 800 square miles. Airbursts the size of Tunguska are estimated to occur every 1,200 years on average. But following the Chelyabinsk meteor, scientists now think the risk of similar objects hitting our planet may be ten times greater than thought previously.

QUESTIONS 1–6

Complete the table below.

Choose **NO MORE THAN TWO NUMBERS AND ONE WORD** *from the passage for each answer.*

Write your answers in spaces 1–6.

The Chelyabinsk meteor strike	The Tunguska meteor strike
The meteor was 10 metres in diameter.	The meteor was **(4)** _____ metres in diameter.
It travelled **(1)** _____ times faster than the speed of sound.	It entered the atmosphere above Russia at about **(5)** _____ per hour.
It exploded **(2)** _____ above the Earth's surface.	It exploded 28,000 feet above the Earth's surface.
It released **(3)** _____ times more energy than the Hiroshima atomic bomb.	It released 185 times more energy than the Hiroshima atomic bomb.
Meteor strikes of this kind occur on average every 10 years.	Meteor strikes of this kind occur on average every **(6)** _____ years.

Questions 7–13

Label the diagram below using words from the box.

*Write the correct letter, **A–G**, in spaces 7–13.*

> **Phases of a meteor strike**
>
> **A** vaporisation of dust and gas
> **B** sub-zero temperature
> **C** fracturing
> **D** dark flight or airburst
> **E** mass loss/fireball
> **F** Earth strike
> **G** deceleration

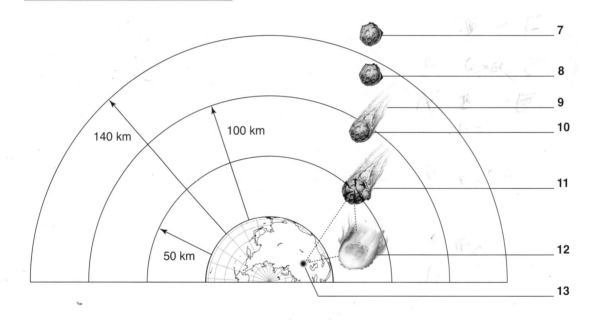

140 km

100 km

50 km

7

8

9

10

11

12

13

10

READING PASSAGE 2

*You should spend about 20 minutes on **Questions 14–26**, which are based on Reading Passage 2 below.*

Some years ago, in 2009, the Mayor of London's advisor on waste questioned the efficiency of recycling, making environmentalists very angry. The chief executive of the independent not-for-profit company Waste and Resources Action Programme (WRAP), Dr Liz Goodwin, responded, saying that the advisor's comments were unhelpful to recycling initiatives and that 'WRAP's independent research, carried out by internationally recognised experts, has shown that across the board recycling is the best environmental option'. Dr Goodwin went on to say: 'Around two thirds of households now recycle as a way of life. The message to householders is that recycling is delivering great environmental benefits and there is absolutely no reason for them to stop.'

However, others can see several reasons to stop recycling, calling the UK's recycling schemes a disorganised waste of time. At the moment recycling means ordinary people sorting out their own waste when it could be dealt with more economically, more efficiently and in a more environmentally friendly way. In the past 20 years in the UK, people have accepted their work as unpaid labourers for councils and waste recycling companies. Every week millions of households diligently sort out their plastic bottles from their glass bottles, their cardboard from their paper, and put it into the correct container. The type and colour of container varies significantly throughout the country; in parts of Scotland you can't recycle aluminium foil but in the south of England the council positively want it. This may seem like a small matter, but it does point to the lack of a coherent strategy for waste disposal. The Chartered Institution of Wastes Management certainly thinks that Britain doesn't have a national strategy. More importantly, if we could count the number of hours spent sorting out recyclable waste – 45 minutes each week by one estimate – and then multiply it by the number of households – 24 million – we get a massive 18 million hours spent each week on recycling.

Other places, however, do things differently. In Maryland, USA, a high-tech system for sorting out waste in a plant and recycling it afterwards increased recycling use by 30 per cent, probably because people did not need to spend three quarters of an hour every week sorting out the waste. There are other issues caused by asking people to give their free time to sort out waste. Because most people generally do not want to do this, local authorities have introduced a range of punishments to deal with them. One is to decrease the regularity of waste collection; another is to check people's rubbish bins and fine them if they put the wrong waste in the wrong bin. Putting paper in the wrong recycling bin cost a journalist from Wales £200.

One reason why questioning the efficiency of recycling makes environmentalists uneasy is that recycling may actually have the opposite effect on the environment. When Britain's waste has been collected, it is sent abroad – to Europe or even longer distances to China – for processing. The cost to the environment of transporting the waste around the world is considerable. But there are alternatives. Firstly, simply using less would help. Secondly, the waste could be buried again in landfill sites around the UK. According to Tim Worstall, in Britain we 'dig up some 110 million cubic metres (mcm) of sand, gravel and clay every year; and each year we produce some 100 mcm of waste'. Unfortunately, the European Union is discouraging landfill by fining countries in the EU who landfill too much. The next alternative is incineration – burning the waste to produce energy. Naturally, incineration is controversial, but burning plastic bottles in power stations to generate electricity saves using fossil fuels like gas, oil and coal. Waste heat produced by the process can be distributed to local public buildings and nearby homes. The question is, which is better environmentally: transporting the waste across the world, or using it locally to produce energy?

Recycling is not a new concept: we have done it for years. We have recycled old cars, scrap metal and paper for a long time now. However, the difference between then and now is that we used to recycle when it made economic sense. Today, it is part of our law and it has somehow become a belief that recycling is the only right thing to do whereas there may be better and more environmentally friendly alternatives. Recycling is not the only answer and the discussion should continue.

Questions 14–17

Choose the correct letter, A, B or C.

14 Current recycling policies mean that
    A taxpayers are working voluntarily to sort waste.
    B recycling takes a lot of time.
    C we make a profit on recycled products.
    D we have to pay too much for recycling.

15 The lack of consistent recycling policies indicates that
    A there are many different recycling processes.
    B there is no overall plan for dealing with waste.
    C recycling is not economical.
    D people are not sorting their waste properly.

16 Which of the following is NOT an alternative to recycling?
    A burying the waste in the ground
    B burning the waste
    C conserving what we use
    D transporting the waste overseas

17 What is one benefit of incineration?
    A The European Union cannot fine the country.
    B Fossil fuels are needed to start the process.
    C The energy produced can be transported across the country.
    D The heat produced can be used to keep some homes warm.

Questions 18–25

Complete the summary below.

Choose NO MORE THAN THREE WORDS from the passage for each answer.

Write your answers in spaces 18–25.

Recycling is widely regarded as the **(18)** _____ for dealing with waste. However, seeing it as the only option ignores the amount of effort it requires and other, possibly better alternatives. It seems that there is no **(19)** _____ for waste disposal. Furthermore, sorting our recyclable waste has a hidden cost. In one US state, waste is sorted in **(20)** _____ waste plants, but in the UK a(n) **(21)** _____ is used to force people to recycle. One method is to make **(22)** _____ less frequent; another is to **(23)** _____ people who place the wrong waste in bins. Alternative ways of dealing with waste could include burying it in **(24)** _____ to replace materials taken out. Another would be **(25)** _____ it for energy.

Question 26

Choose the correct letter, A, B or C.

26 What is the best title for the article?

   A Why people hate recycling

   B Economical alternatives to recycling

   C Recycling and the law

   D The real cost of recycling

READING PASSAGE 3

You should spend about 20 minutes on Questions 27–40, which are based on Reading Passage 3 below.

Hello 3D printing, goodbye China

A A spectre is haunting the great container ship ports of China, with their highways jammed by lorries and the vast factory estates stretching from the coast of the South China Sea to the mountainous inland provinces. It is the spectre of a revolution led by a quiet, software-driven 3D printer, a machine that can laser up layers of liquid or granular resin or even cell tissue into a finished product. Some 3D printers are huge devices that make complete components such as aircraft parts. Others are small units that could stand next to a desk and create a small plastic prototype. Maplin, the British electronics retailer, said last week it would start selling one for just £700. The Velleman K8200 will allow those who are so inclined to make simple objects — mobile phone covers, perhaps, or toys. 'The only restriction is your imagination. You can make whatever you want,' said Pieter Nartus, export manager at Velleman.

B To visionaries in the West, the digital 3D printer promises to disrupt conventional manufacturing and supply chains so radically that advocates compare its impact to the advent of the production line or the internet. In China, whose big factories are thinking of using giant 3D printers for manufacturing, the technology does not seem to pose an immediate threat. 'It is on their horizon but it is not a factor right now,' says a British buying agent who sources plastics in China. However, as Chinese leaders ought to know from their compulsory classes in Karl Marx, control of the means of production is everything. And if 3D printing takes off, production will come back to a place near you.

C The implications, economists say, are limitless. No huge factories. No fleets of trucks. No ships. No supply chain. No tariffs. Few middlemen. Orders tailored exactly to demand, so no need for stock and warehouses. Just a printer, raw materials, software and a design. The advantages do not end there. Because the item is 'sintered' – created from a powdered material – to precise settings using a laser, there is no waste such as metal shavings. To customise a product, the user simply changes the software. An operator presses a button and the printer spits out the item.

D 'The first implication is that more goods will be manufactured at or closer to their point of purchase or consumption,' said Richard D'Aveni, a professor at Dartmouth College in the USA. Writing in the *Harvard Business Review*, D'Aveni predicted the elimination of the long supply chain linked to a huge factory staffed by cheap workers and sited on the other side of the world. It may be the most significant, if underplayed, article in that distinguished publication in decades. 'China has grabbed outsourced manufacturing contracts from every mature economy by pushing the mass-manufacturing model to its limit,' he wrote. 'It not only aggregates enough demand to create unprecedented efficiencies of scale but also minimises a key cost: labour. … Under a model of widely distributed, highly flexible small-scale manufacturing, these daunting advantages become liabilities. No workforce can be paid little enough to make up for the costs of shipping across oceans.'

E   In the brutal war for margin amid volatile commodities and currencies at the bottom end of the market, where China has carved its niche, the numbers tell their own ominous story. In a world of 3D manufacturing, the classic supply chain makes no commercial sense. 'China won't be a loser in the new era,' D'Aveni argued in the *Harvard Business Review*. 'It will have a domestic market to serve . . . and its domestic market is huge. But China will have to give up on being the mass-manufacturing powerhouse of the world.'

F   China, of course, is not sitting still. It is eagerly buying Western 3D printing technology and making its own lightweight machines to sell to consumers. The Ministry of Industry and Information Technology has already allocated £20 million to fund 10 research centres and set up a group of 40 participating companies. So there is no doubt about China's scientific, engineering and intellectual commitment to 3D manufacturing. However, it is a fundamentally different concept in China. To the Chinese, it is an industrial tool to be used in making more things to sell. To Western economies that are hooked on cheap imports with a huge carbon footprint, it could be a means of transformation – perhaps even an agent of de-industrialisation.

Questions 27–32

*Reading Passage 3 has six paragraphs, **A–F**.*

*Which paragraph, **A–F**, contains the following information?*

*Write the correct letter, **A–F**, next to Questions 27–32.*

27 a change in China's markets

28 the advent of a new technology

29 a description of the new business model

30 a comparison of 3D printing with past innovations

31 China's investments in 3D printing

32 possible future consequences of 3D printing

Questions 33–37

Classify the following as said by

  A *Pieter Nartus*

  B *Karl Marx*

  C *Richard D'Aveni*

*Write the correct letter, **A**, **B** or **C**, next to Questions 33–37.*

33 China will not manufacture products for the world in the future.

34 There will be no advantages in efficiencies of scale.

35 Control over how we produce things counts for everything.

36 What we make will be limited only by our imagination.

37 Goods will be made closer to the consumer.

Questions 38–40

Choose the correct letter A, B, C or D.

38 Which is NOT an advantage of 3D printing?

C

   A You do not need to buy stock.

   B You do not need to store materials in large buildings.

   C Goods are made from powder. *○*

   D There is no waste.

39 How did China achieve industrial growth?

B

   A It had manufacturing contracts. *○*

   B It had low labour costs.

   C There was high demand for its products from one area.

   D The cost of shipping goods across the oceans was not significant.

40 What does the writer think about China's reaction to 3D printing?

A

   A Chinese business leaders do not fully realise the implications.

   B China should be investing more in it.

   C China should concentrate more on its domestic market.

   D The changes will leave China behind. *○*

WRITING TASK 1

You should spend about 20 minutes on this task.

> *The infographics below show employment statistics for UK residents by English language proficiency in 2013.*
>
> *Summarise the information by selecting and reporting the main features, and make comparisons where relevant.*

**25.7 million
people (aged 16–64) were in employment**

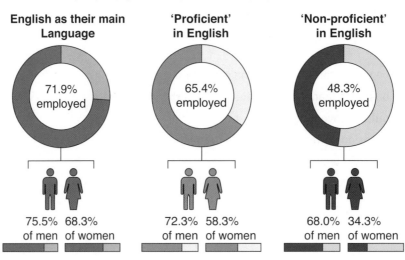

English as their main Language

71.9% employed

75.5% of men   68.3% of women

'Proficient' in English

65.4% employed

72.3% of men   58.3% of women

'Non-proficient' in English

48.3% employed

68.0% of men   34.3% of women

**Of those in employment
the most common occupations were:**

English as their main Language

17.7% Professional   13.2% Technical

'Proficient' in English

19.2% Elementary   17.1% Professional

'Non-proficient' in English

38.2% Elementary   21.1% Skilled trades

Write at least 150 words.

WRITING TASK 2

You should spend about 40 minutes on this task.

Write about the following topic:

> Some people think that taxation should be kept to a minimum as the money people earn should be theirs to do with as they wish. Others believe that people should pay a significant level of tax in order to support the public services we all depend on.
>
> In your view, what is the fairest way to deal with the issue of taxation?

Give reasons for your answer and include any relevant examples from your own knowledge or experience.

Write at least 250 words.

PART 1: Introduction and interview

Listen to Track 26, pressing pause after each question to answer.

26

PART 2: Individual long turn

Before you read the task card, listen to Track 27.

27

Describe a person who has had a big influence on you.

You should say
    who this person was
    when you met the person
    what the person was like
and say what the person did that made them so significant in your life.

PART 3: Two-way discussion

Listen to Track 28, pressing pause after each question to answer.

28

SECTION 1   *Questions 1–14*

Read the advertisement below and answer Questions 1–7.

UniReady

UniReady are specialist suppliers of student essentials. We supply a range of products, including bedding, cooking equipment, cleaning products and personal hygiene products. Orders are delivered directly to your hall of residence at very competitive prices.

Luxury Bedroom, Bathroom & Kitchen Pack (Single)

This luxury pack truly has everything. It is perfect for anyone who wants the best waiting for them on arrival. It is great value for money and you can begin settling in and making friends without having to worry about shopping for these essential items. This pack is for single beds. Items are available in a variety of colours.

Luxury Bedding Pack
- Single superior duvet
- Pillow
- Single fitted sheet

Luxury Bath Pack
- Face cloth
- Hand towel
- Bath towel
- Bathroom pack
  (soap, shampoo & conditioner)
- Hangers x10

Luxury Utensil Pack
- Corkscrew
- Tin opener
- Vegetable peeler
- Wooden spoon

Luxury Crockery Pack
- Knife & fork
- Dessert spoon
- Teaspoon
- Dinner plate
- Side plate
- Cereal bowl
- Mug
- Glass tumbler

Luxury Extra Pack
- Chopping board
- 6-piece wooden knife block

Essentials Pack

This pack is right for anyone in catered accommodation or for someone who is in a shared flat and just wants the basics to be there on arrival. We even give you a free bathroom pack to help you clean up before you head off to meet all your new uni mates.

Essentials Bedding Pack
- Single duvet
- Pillow
- Single fitted sheet

Essentials Bath Pack
- Soap, shampoo & conditioner

Essentials Crockery Pack
- Knife & fork
- Dessert spoon
- Teaspoon
- Dinner plate
- Side plate
- Cereal bowl
- Mug
- Glass tumbler

If you would like your items to be delivered by a recorded service, this can be done at a cost of £6.00 to an address provided by you. If you are not able to be at home to receive this delivery, it can be left at the reception desk at your halls of residence.

Questions 1–7

Look at the advertisement on pages 115–116.

Do the following statements agree with the information given in the advertisement?
Write

TRUE	*if the statement agrees with the information*
FALSE	*if the statement contradicts the information*
NOT GIVEN	*if there is no information on this*

Example	*Answer*
It is too expensive to have orders delivered to a hall of residence.	**FALSE**

1   The Luxury Pack is suitable for any kind of bed.

2   The Luxury Pack includes items used in preparing food.

3   You can choose from four colours if you buy the Luxury Pack.

4   The Essentials Pack contains something to sleep under.

5   The cereal bowls are made of plastic.

6   Your pack can be delivered even if you are not at home.

7   The Luxury Pack includes two bath towels.

8   The Essentials Pack is for students who live with other people.

Read the information below and answer Questions 9–14.

Shawlands Literary Festival

A Adventure thrillers

Two of our bestselling writers of adventure novels for young adults, Sophie Galliano and Robert McKenzie, talk about their writing. Galliano discusses her action-packed new novel, *Second Chance,* and McKenzie introduces his new thriller, *Tribal Fissure*. Both authors write stories full of excitement and adventure – now is your chance to hear how.

B Cold War stories

Bestselling author Jed Mack tells the story of one of the most notorious spies in US history. During the Cold War the spy, Tony Houghton, passed top secret information on to the enemy and even betrayed his closest friends and fellow agents working undercover in the USSR. Using newly released information, and with help from Houghton's former colleagues, Mack tells a story of secrecy, trust and betrayal.

C Conversations with poets

You will have the rare opportunity to hear award-winning Jamaican poet Goldy Fritzberg in conversation with fellow poet and the festival's creative writing director, Penny Worcester, about their work.

D Cartoon workshop

Make sure that you join our workshop with the brilliant artist Roger Nial. Come and learn some of his tips for creating comic characters and zany stories. Although mainly aimed at older children, there is plenty of inspirational family fun for everyone, so sign up and make your own comic creation.

E Lost Civilisation

Writer Rab Greenham explains how he learnt of the lost world of the Maya, their gods, their art and their knowledge of science. Travelling around Central America, Greenham explored the background of a culture now lost to history. In this session, you can hear about the various adventures Greenham had while he was gathering material for his book.

F How to write for the stage

Dramaturge Keith O'Reilly gives a masterclass in stage writing. The author of several award-winning stage dramas, O'Reilly explores the art of writing dialogue and plots in an unmissable session.

G Word salad

Would you like to combine two of your favourite things? Eva Katic explores the connection between our appetites and our love of words with a talk about food poetry. She also invites her audience to bring along some of their favourite recipes to help the evening along.

H Every Stone a God

Grayson Hinds has been chosen as one of the best young writers of the year. In this session she talks about her new novel, *Every Stone a God,* a powerful story of love and friendship during the Second World War. A young woman is living a bohemian lifestyle in Germany when a visiting professor takes her under his wing. Their friendship develops into love – and a frightening dilemma for both.

Questions 9–14

Look at the literature festival programme on page 117.

*For which sessions, **A–H**, are the following statements true?*

*Write the correct letter, **A–H**, next to Questions 9–14. Note: There are more three sessions than you will need.*

9 Children between the ages of ten and twelve who are interested in drawing would be interested in this session.

10 This session is for people who like historical fiction.

11 You should go to this session if you would like to learn how to write plays.

12 Teenagers who like action novels would be interested in this session.

13 This session is about a non-fiction book about a particular part of the world.

14 People interested in hearing fellow writers talking to each other about their work should attend this session.

SECTION 2   *Questions 15–26*

Read the information below and answer Questions 15–26.

University Curling: equipment, players and basic rules

Equipment

- All equipment will be provided, including stones. Take care of the stones. They are extremely heavy and should never be lifted. Stones (also called rocks) should not be thrown overly hard and should always be stopped using your brush, not your foot, otherwise they may injure you or knock you over. Curling stones are expensive and replacement costs exceed £800 per stone.
- Players must wear appropriate clothing – the arena can be chilly. Wear warm, loose-fitting clothing; gloves and hats are optional.
- Lockers are free of charge, but you must bring your own lock.

Club rules

- A valid student card must be brought to the game and produced on request. The sports manager will frequently check players' student cards. Failure to produce a valid card will automatically lead to a player being disqualified.
- No street shoes are permitted on the arena surface. You must wear a clean pair of shoes.
- Alcohol consumption is not permitted during games.

Sports carding system

A card system has been created to promote an enjoyable atmosphere for all participants. Officials and/or sports managers may issue either a yellow or a red card to any participant before, during or after a contest for inappropriate conduct. Team captains are responsible for making sure their team mates understand the carding system and play by the rules.

Yellow cards may be issued for:
* bad language
* arguing with officials or supervisors
* delaying the game
* failure to comply with equipment regulations

Red cards (immediate game ejection) may be issued for:
* offensive language and/or behaviour to an official or other player
* physical threats or physical violence directed at an official or other player
* fighting of any sort

Game rules

* Each team consists of 4–8 players and can include any combination of males and females. A minimum of three players is needed to start a game.
* Score cards are provided by the sports manager. Both captains must sign the score card at the end of the game.
* If there is a dispute, the sports manager will make a decision. That decision is final.
* Games last for 6 ends or rounds or 2 hours, whichever finishes first. Games start at 8:30 p.m. Please be at the sports club a quarter of an hour prior to the game starting.
* The winner of a coin toss has the option of playing first or second. The loser gets to choose the colour of stones.
* A team scores one point for each stone that slides nearer the centre circle than any stone of the opposing team.
* Players must not throw two stones towards each other or engage in any other negligent behaviour. Failure to comply with these rules will result in a team being automatically ejected from the league, and the team may be liable for any damage that occurs as a result.

Game details

* Curling stones: When you throw a stone down the ice, it will curl, or bend, one way or another depending on how the player has thrown it and how much rotation they have applied to it. How much (or little) a stone curls also depends on the conditions of the playing surface and the actions of the team players who are sweeping the ice in front of the stone.
* Sweeping: Sweeping before the stone makes it curl less and travel further. Captains don't sweep stones frequently; they are responsible for their team's strategy.

Questions 15–20

Look at the information leaflet on pages 119–120.

Do the following statements agree with the information given in the information leaflet?
Write

TRUE	*if the statement agrees with the information*
FALSE	*if the statement contradicts the information*
NOT GIVEN	*if there is no information on this*

15 You should wear clothing that keeps you cool.

16 Lockers are available in three sizes.

17 You may be asked to provide your student card.

18 You can only go on the arena surface if you are wearing special curling shoes.

19 Players who behave badly will be fined.

20 Players can be sent off for hitting another person.

Questions 21–26

Complete the sentences below.

*Choose **NO MORE THAN TWO WORDS** or **A NUMBER** from the leaflet for each answer.*

21 Each game takes _____ or six rounds.

22 The player who wins the _____ can choose which team starts the game.

23 The direction of the stone can be curled, depending upon how it is thrown, how much
_____ a player gives it, and other factors.

24 Team players can make the stone travel further by _____ in front of it.

25 Points are scored for getting stones near the _____ of the target.

26 The captain tells team members how they should play and also decides on the team's
_____.

Read the article below and answer Questions 27–40.

The Mozart Effect

In 1993 Frances Rauscher and Gordon Shaw conducted an experiment in which a group of students listened to Mozart's Sonata for Two Pianos in D Major for 10 minutes prior to doing an IQ test. Their results showed a temporary increase in their IQ scores. The media picked up on this and called it 'the Mozart effect'. The discovery had an immediate social and political effect, with the Governor of Georgia, USA, spending $105,000 to give every family in the state a recording of Mozart's music to play to their children.

However, using music in the interest of health has had a long history. Prior to Rauscher and Shaw's experiment, Dr Alfred Tomatis, a French ear, nose and throat specialist, pioneered using music in the treatment of children with speech and communication disorders such as autism or dyslexia. He found that music made a difference in their treatment. Tomatis started to look at the anatomy of sound and how it affects the brain. But why did he choose Mozart instead of other composers?

First of all, Tomatis distinguished between listening and hearing; hearing is seen as a passive process where sounds flood into our awareness, whereas listening is an active process that can be trained. Secondly, he believed that high-frequency sounds stimulate connections between the ear and the central nervous system, and playing music that contains high-frequency sounds is one of the ways we can train children to listen better. Consequently, some pieces of music are better than others and Tomatis found that Mozart's music contains lots of high-frequency sounds. Thus, he thought that Mozart's music could be used in the treatment of certain conditions.

Although other studies have not been able to replicate the original research of Tomatis and Rauscher and Shaw, the idea that music can be an aid to learning has not disappeared. In fact, other studies seem to show that music does have a positive effect on children with communication and learning difficulties. At Aberdare Boys School, Anne Savan taught children with special needs, 'They lacked co-ordination,' she said. 'They were often frustrated with the tasks set for them and became aggressive. The whole thing was a stressful situation.' Savan had been playing background music to the children for five months, and then by chance she played Mozart to them. Almost immediately the children became calmer and more productive. On observing this and making sure it was not an accident, Savan set up a research project with the University of Reading. They measured children's physiological signs (blood pressure, body temperature, respiration and pulse rate) when music was played at the start of a lesson, 20 minutes into the lesson and one hour after the lesson had finished in order to create a profile.

Savan found a 10 per cent drop in the physiological parameters when music was played after 20 minutes. She started by playing Mozart to the children and then progressed to other music, but found that other music produced no statistically significant response. The next thing she tried was to play different Mozart pieces but found that not all his music had an effect: only orchestral music without piano or human voice produced a response. She then looked at the structure of the music and its rhythm: she sped up the music and slowed it down but the children's physiological signs stayed unchanged. She then went on to look at the patterns within the music: she played the music backwards to the children but with only little effect. Like Tomatis before her, Savan experimented with the frequency; she took out the high frequencies and low frequencies in turn but had only a poor response, and concluded that a combination of factors are needed to produce the response.

In an attempt to pin down which combination of factors could be responsible for the effect, in 2001 John Hughes analysed the periodicity, or patterns, in Mozart's music. He found that Mozart's music contained a high level of repetition of patterns within 10–60 seconds of each other. The Sonata for Two Pianos in D Major certainly does contain repetition of musical patterns and phrases as the two pianos play patterns and reply to each other. Unfortunately, despite the promise of early studies and investigations into whether it is the high frequencies within the music, its rhythm or patterns, no direct link has yet been established to definitely prove that the Mozart effect truly exists.

Questions 27–34

Look at the article on pages 122–123.

Do the following statements agree with the information given in the article?
Write

TRUE	if the statement agrees with the information
FALSE	if the statement contradicts the information
NOT GIVEN	if there is no information on this

27 The announcement of Rauscher and Shaw's findings had an immediate effect on teaching methods.

28 Using music to treat patients is a relatively new practice.

29 Tomatis looked at the reasons for the popularity of certain kinds of music.

30 Tomatis believed that people can be trained to hear.

31 Other studies have been able to confirm the findings of Rauscher and Shaw.

32 Savan's students became calmer when she played Mozart to them.

33 Savan measured children's physiological signs at regular intervals.

34 Hughes looked at the repetition of patterns in Mozart's music.

Questions 35–40

Look at the actions Savan carried out in her study below.

*Write the correct letter, **A**, **B** or **C**, next to Questions 35–40.*

    A The action had a positive effect on listeners.
    B The action had a slight effect on listeners.
    C The action had no effect on listeners.

35 playing Mozart

36 playing other music

37 playing Mozart's instrumental pieces

38 playing the music faster or slower

39 reversing the music

40 removing some sound frequencies

WRITING

WRITING TASK 1

You should spend about 20 minutes on this task.

> *You recently purchased an item of furniture that was faulty. You telephoned the shop about the problem(s) and were asked to put your complaint in writing.*
>
> *Write a letter to the shop. In your letter*
> - *explain what the problem(s) is/are*
> - *explain if anything was done to improve the situation*
> - *say what you would like the shop to do.*

Write at least 150 words. You do NOT need to write any addresses.

Begin your letter as follows:

Dear Sir or Madam,

WRITING TASK 2

You should spend about 40 minutes on this task.

Write about the following topic:

> *Some people think any form of experimentation on animals for any reason is wrong. They believe all such experiments should be banned. Others think the benefits research offers us in terms of medical advances make experiments on animals worthwhile.*
>
> *Discuss both views and give your opinion.*

Give reasons for your answer and include any relevant examples from your own knowledge or experience.

Write at least 250 words.

General Training Test B

SECTION 1   Questions 1–14

Read the information below and answer Questions 1–14.

Fundraising Ideas 3: Car Boot Sale

A   Car boot sales are a great way to raise money. Even if you don't have a lot of things you don't need, you can ask your friends and family to do a clear-out and give you their unwanted items to help you raise money. Spring is a great time to hold a car boot sale, before everyone goes on holiday and the days get too hot.

B   Many people have found this a great way to start their fundraising; it doesn't take a lot of preparation and can raise quite a lot of money in one day. In the past volunteers have raised between £50 and £100 from one car boot sale; you could easily make £200–300 by doing two or three car boot sales if you have a lot of stuff to sell.

C   Lots of websites advertise dates for car boot sales. Look at <u>Your Car Booty</u> and <u>Car Boot Junction</u> – websites that list boot sales across the UK. Otherwise, you can pick up your local newspaper or search for 'car boot sales' near you on the internet.

D   Look in your garage, shed or attic. If you are not much of a collector, then contact your family and friends to see if they can give you anything to sell. Tell people about the sale through Facebook and Twitter. You could also put up an advert in your local shop asking people to donate their unwanted goods. Tell them it's for a good cause.

E   Have a clear-out of all of your stuff, from clothes to furniture. In my house, the garage, shed and loft are normally great places to start! If you're not much of a hoarder, then it's a great idea to contact your friends and family members and see if they have anything you could sell. You can sell pretty much anything at boot sales, including clothing, books, jewellery, CDs, DVDs, games, furniture and kitchen items. Some car boot sales will also let you sell cakes or other food items (but make sure you check first); this can be a great boost to your fundraising and may attract people to your stall too!

F First of all, tell the place holding the car boot sale that you are selling for a good cause – they may offer a lower pitch price for stalls raising money for charity. Next, work out the prices for your items in advance, and either put stickers on them or put a sign up, for example 'All CDs £2'. Advertise that you are raising money for charity, and if people try to bargain you down on your prices, remind them you are raising money for a good cause. They may want to go with the higher price. Finally, check whether tables are provided. If not, you will need to remember to pack one.

G Tip 1: Put your alarm clock on! Car boot sales often start early. Take some hot coffee/tea/chocolate and dress up warm; you will probably be standing outside for a couple of hours!

Tip 2: Early in the car boot sale, you will have people wanting to buy your items at a cheap price. They will then put them on their own stall to sell at a higher price so don't sell all your items too early. Try to have a friend help you in the first couple of hours of the sale.

Tip 3: Say no when people haggle with you if you think the price they are offering is too low.

Questions 1–6

The text on pages 126–127 has seven sections, A–G.

Choose the correct heading for sections B–G from the list of headings below.

Write the correct number, i–ix, next to Questions 1–6.

List of Headings
i What can you sell?
ii Where can you sell?
iii What happens on the day?
iv When is a good time for a car boot sale?
v How much do car boot sales cost?
vi How can you start?
vii Why do a car boot sale?
viii Who goes to car boot sales?
ix What do I need to do to prepare?

Example	*Answer*
Section **A**	**iv**

1 Section **B**

2 Section **C**

3 Section **D**

4 Section **E**

5 Section **F**

6 Section **G**

Questions 7–14

Do the following statements agree with the information given in the text?

Write

TRUE	*if the statement agrees with the information*
FALSE	*if the statement contradicts the information*
NOT GIVEN	*if there is no information on this*

7   Spring is a good time for a car boot sale because of the holidays.

8   Car boot sales raise £75 on average.

9   You could ask people close to you to give you things to sell.

10   You can sell vehicles at car boot sales.

11   If you are selling things for charity, you may get a discount from the organisers.

12   The organisers always provide tables to put things on.

13   Other sellers will often try to buy your items and then sell them at their table.

14   You should accept all offers to buy something.

Staff training events

A Efficiency training

A better understanding of time management and time management techniques can make you more effective in your work, enabling you to achieve more in fewer hours and giving you time to relax properly. This course is a blend of online materials that will let you try things out before you have a short face-to-face session.

B Performance review for reviewees

As an employee, it is your responsibility to get the best out of your work so that your team functions at its full potential. This course will develop the skills you need to understand your performance review and focuses on the company policies which must guide you in your work. Presentation, DVD and group discussion will be used to give you an opportunity to practise in a supportive environment.

C Health and safety

This online course provides basic information about health and safety in the company and helps you to understand your responsibility to keep yourself safe, look out for the safety of others, and co-operate with other departments in the company in an emergency.

D Diversity and equality training

The company aims to provide a work environment free from unfairness. The course focuses on the law and people's rights, and looks at how we can accept and celebrate our differences. Improving our workplace culture can often be challenging, so the first step is to increase our knowledge, understanding and skills in this area.

E IT systems and remote working

Managing an effective team can be difficult even when the team is based in the same office, but when team members are working in different locations sometimes even based abroad, management becomes a real challenge. Remote working is on the increase and managers need all the help they can get to make it work. This course will enable you to deal with remote working, ensuring that your team feels motivated and integrated.

Questions 15–19

Look at the text on page 130.

*Which event, **A–E**, is the most suitable for people's training needs?*

*Write the correct number, **i–viii**, next to Questions 15–20. Note: There are more training needs than events so you will not use them all.*

i	You need to prepare for your yearly appraisal and would like to know what happens.
ii	You are not good at meeting deadlines.
iii	You would like more people to work flexibly from home.
iv	You need to know about the law regarding equal opportunities.
v	You would like to learn more about computers and improve your word processing skills.
vi	You would like to know about working with international colleagues.
vii	You would like to learn first aid.
viii	You have to learn about the possible dangers at work.

15 A Efficiency training

16 B Performance review for reviewees

17 C Health and safety

18 D Diversity and equality training

19 E IT systems and remote working

Questions 20–25

Read the text below and answer questions 20–25.

Applying for staff development funds

The company sees staff development as a priority and is committed to developing the experience, knowledge and ability of all staff regardless of position within the organisation.

The company has an annual budget for staff development, and staff are encouraged to apply for funds for training relevant to their job or any training identified in their yearly performance review. While it may be appropriate for some staff members to attend more than one training session, there is a limit of three sessions per year per staff member.

Funding should always be approved prior to incurring costs. This is to ensure that we are able to monitor the staff development budget. It also ensures that staff can be reimbursed for expenses. Without approval, there is a risk that a staff member will personally have to bear the cost of any training he or she has had.

The approval process:

1   Speak to your line manager about the training for which you would like to apply for funding. Afterwards, please make sure you have the agreement in writing so that the Staff Development Manager and Financial Officer are able to find evidence of the agreement in case any problems occur.

2   On agreement, you will need to complete a staff development form and submit it to the Staff Development Manager. He/She will review your application and reply within one week of receiving it. It is important to wait for signed approval before proceeding further. You will receive a staff development cost code on approval. You will need this for the next stage.

3   After approval, and in advance of any expenditure, you may need to complete a purchase request order. Send the purchase request to the finance office, and remember to include your staff development cost code. The finance office will then book travel tickets and/or make any payments so that staff members do not need to spend their own money. It is important to make sure you have allowed enough time for the finance office to process the purchase request.

4   Expense claims: In a situation where the time between applying for funding and sending in a purchase order and the date of the training or event is very short, a staff member may pay for the event themselves and then claim back the cost through an expense claim. Please note: you will still need to present a staff development form and have it approved before submitting an expense claim. You will also need a staff development cost code from your approved staff development form to complete a claim.

Questions 20–22

Do the following statements agree with the information given in the text?

Write

> **TRUE**   *if the statement agrees with the information*
> **FALSE**   *if the statement contradicts the information*
> **NOT GIVEN**   *if there is no information on this*

20 There is an unlimited amount of money for staff development.

21 You can apply for funding to go to a conference.

22 You are discouraged from spending your own money.

Questions 23–25

Complete the flowchart.

*Choose **NO MORE THAN THREE WORDS** from the text for each answer.*

Write your answers in spaces 23–25.

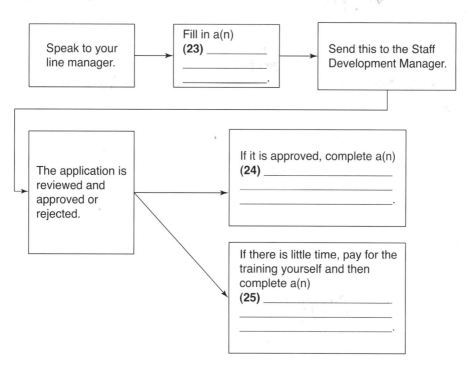

Read the article below and answer Questions 26–40.

Fracking

Fracking refers to a technique for extracting natural gas from shale deep within the earth. Fracking is shorthand for 'hydraulic fracturing' and refers to how shale rock is fractured apart by injecting a mixture of water and chemicals into it at very high pressure. Fracking for shale gas has become big business in the United States, where the search for energy is one of the country's main concerns. However, the procedure is controversial and has as many opponents as supporters.

Fracking is not a new technique. It was first used in the 1860s, and then used industrially in 1949. However, as the oil reserves in America decreased and energy sources from abroad became more expensive, gas trapped in shale became an attractive commercial proposition. Shale gas is natural gas, or methane, trapped in tiny pockets in shale rock formations. Shale rock is a form of mudstone formed between 252 and 66 million years ago. It is distinguishable because it is laminated (made up of thin layers) and fissile (it can be split into thin layers). For the energy industry, black shale is important because it is the source rock for many of the world's most important oil and gas reserves. Black shale gets its colour from organic matter that was deposited along with the mud from which the shale formed. As the mud was compressed and warmed within the earth, the organic material was transformed into oil and natural gas.

In order to extract shale gas, a shaft, or well, is drilled to over one mile deep into the earth and then horizontally into the shale rock. The vertical well is then encased in steel and/or cement. After that, water needs to be delivered to the site: this can be up to 200 tanker trucks. The water is mixed with sand and chemicals and a pumper truck injects this hydraulic fluid into the shaft at high pressure, causing the shale to crack, or fracture. The sand in the mixture keeps the cracks open, allowing gas to flow to the surface into storage tanks. The gas is then piped to users. Meanwhile, water recovered from the shaft is stored in open pits before being taken to a treatment plant for recycling and eventual reuse. After all the gas has been collected, the shaft is sealed off with concrete to make sure that the injected hydraulic fluid cannot escape into water supplies.

An estimated 250 billion cubic metres of natural gas were brought to the surface using this method in the US in 2013. Since the US government gave out licenses to companies, its carbon emissions have gone down. Indeed, fracking has quite a few things going for it. This is because natural gas is far cleaner to burn than oil or coal in power stations. Furthermore, the area occupied by a fracking well is much smaller than a conventional oil well. So the question is, if fracking is so simple, clean and efficient, why are people concerned about it?

The problem is in the method used to get the gas out. The chemicals in the hydraulic fluid are toxic, consisting of a mixture of lubricants, poisons to stop bacteria growing in the pipes, and hydrochloric acid to dissolve unwanted cement in the pipes. This chemical mix finds its way to the surface through accidents at well-heads, fluids flowing back to the surface and leaks in the system. There is also the economical and environmental cost of transporting and using water – between three and five million gallons of water are needed to fracture a seam.

Furthermore, some experts think that fracking may be linked to the occurrence of earthquakes – earthquakes of magnitude 2.7 on the Richter scale have been increasing near Oklahoma City, an area where gas has been extracted using the technique. But perhaps the most persuasive argument is that fracking simply prolongs our over-reliance on carbon-based fuels, when we should be moving to technologies that do not produce carbon emissions or that are not harmful to the environment, such as solar energy, wind or wave power. In effect, fracking does not deal with the real issue of how we can produce energy without harming the environment. However, many people think fracking could be America's bridge between the carbon-based energy systems of the past and a cleaner way of producing energy in the future.

Questions 26–32

Do the following statements agree with the information given in the article?

Write

TRUE	*if the statement agrees with the information*
FALSE	*if the statement contradicts the information*
NOT GIVEN	*if there is no information on this*

26 Fracking was first used commercially in 1949.

27 Natural gas is formed from organic material in shale rock.

28 The organic material in shale comes from organisms that lived in sea water.

29 Sand is used in fracking to keep fissures open.

30 Fracking is clean, simple and efficient.

31 Fracking involves the use of harmless chemicals.

32 Chemicals injected into the shale rock stay there.

Questions 33–36

Read the third paragraph again and complete the diagram.

*Choose **NO MORE THAN TWO WORDS** from the article for each answer.*

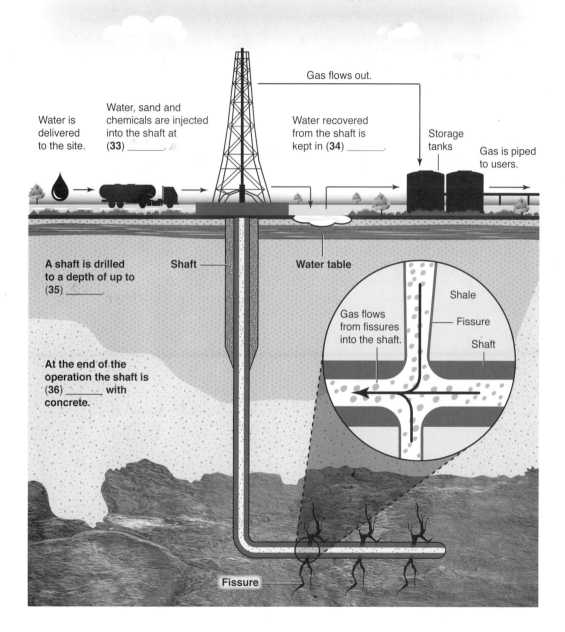

Gas flows out.

Water is delivered to the site.

Water, sand and chemicals are injected into the shaft at (33) _____.

Water recovered from the shaft is kept in (34) _____.

Storage tanks

Gas is piped to users.

A shaft is drilled to a depth of up to (35) _____.

Shaft

Water table

Gas flows from fissures into the shaft.

Shale

Fissure

Shaft

At the end of the operation the shaft is (36) _____ with concrete.

Fissure

Questions 37–40

Complete the summary of the final paragraph below.

*Choose **NO MORE THAN TWO WORDS** from the article for each answer.*

Opponents of fracking believe that **(37)** _____ may be caused by the process. In addition, they claim that fracking encourages the United States' **(38)** _____ on fossil fuels. They say that fracking does not help us to tackle the **(39)** _____ but it may act as a **(40)** _____ from carbon-based energy to green energy production.

WRITING TASK 1

You should spend about 20 minutes on this task.

> *A friend from another country is planning to visit your country in October or November for a week.*
>
> *Write a letter to your friend. In your letter*
> - *recommend a city or town they could visit and give reasons for your recommendations*
> - *say what clothes they may need to bring at that time of year*
> - *suggest meeting your friend while they are in your country.*

Write at least 150 words. You do NOT need to write any addresses.

Begin your letter as follows:

Dear ...,

WRITING TASK 2

You should spend about 40 minutes on this task.

Write about the following topic:

> *Today more people are shopping online than ever before.*
>
> *Why do people choose to shop in this way?*
>
> *Are there disadvantages to shopping online?*

Give reasons for your answer and include any relevant examples from your own knowledge or experience.

Write at least 250 words.

Mini-dictionary

Some of the more difficult words from each of the Listening and Reading texts are defined here in this mini-dictionary. The definitions focus on the meanings of the words in the context in which they appear in the text. Definitions and examples are from *Collins COBUILD Key Words for IELTS (Advanced), Collins COBUILD IELTS Dictionary* and *Collins COBUILD Advanced Dictionary.*

TEST 1: LISTENING

Section 1

confirmation /ˌkɒnfɜːˈmeɪʃən/ NOUN **Confirmation** of an arrangement or appointment is a statement that it is definite, for example in an email or on the telephone. • *Confirmation of my order arrived by email.*

Section 2

designated /ˈdezɪgneɪtəd/ ADJECTIVE A **designated** place or thing has been set aside for a particular purpose. • *Smoking is only permitted in designated areas.*

motivated /ˈmoʊtɪveɪtəd/ ADJECTIVE A **motivated** person is very keen to do something, especially to work hard or to succeed. • *...highly motivated employees.*

suite /swiːt/ (**suites**) NOUN A **suite** is a set of rooms set aside for a particular purpose. • *The facilities include an arts centre, library and IT suite.*

Section 3

potential /pəˈtenʃəl/ ADJECTIVE You use **potential** to say that someone or something could possibly become the particular kind of person or thing mentioned. • *The company has identified 60 potential customers.*

prominent /ˈprɒmɪnənt/ ADJECTIVE Something that is **prominent** is very noticeable or is an important part of something else. • *Here the window plays a prominent part in the design.*

sector /ˈsektə/ (**sectors**) NOUN A particular **sector** of a country's economy is the part connected with that specified type of industry. • *...the nation's manufacturing sector.*

Section 4

apply /əˈplaɪ/ (**applies, applying, applied**) VERB Something such as a remark or name that **is applied to** something is used to refer to it or describe it. • *...a biological term that cannot be applied to a whole culture.*

comprehensive /ˌkɒmprɪˈhensɪv/ ADJECTIVE Something that is **comprehensive** includes everything that is needed or relevant. • *The first step involves a comprehensive analysis of the job.*

consume /kənˈsjuːm/, US /-ˈsuːm/ (**consumes, consuming, consumed**) VERB [FORMAL] If you **consume** something, you eat or drink it. • *Martha would consume nearly a pound of cheese per day.*

deposit /dɪˈpɒzɪt/ (**deposits, depositing, deposited**) VERB If a substance **is deposited** somewhere, it is left there as a result of a chemical or geological process. • *The phosphate was deposited by the decay of marine microorganisms.*

evidence /ˈevɪdəns/ NOUN **Evidence** is anything that you see, experience, read or are told that causes you to believe that something is true or has really happened. • *There is a lot of evidence that stress is partly responsible for disease.*

excavate /ˈekskəveɪt/ (**excavates, excavating, excavated**) VERB When archaeologists or other people **excavate** things such as pots, bones or buildings, they find them by carefully digging and removing earth in an area of land, in order to discover information about the past. • *Archaeologists excavated the skeletal remains in Indonesia.*

incorporate /ɪnˈkɔːpəreɪt/ (**incorporates, incorporating, incorporated**) VERB [FORMAL] If one thing **incorporates** another thing, it includes the other thing as part of it. • *Many sports garments now incorporate technology which helps to carry any sweat away from the body.*

native /ˈneɪtɪv/ ADJECTIVE Plants or animals that are **native to** a particular region live or grow there naturally and were not brought there. • *...a project to create a 50-acre forest of native Caledonian pines.*

roam /rəʊm/ (**roams, roaming, roamed**) VERB If a person or animal **roams**, they travel around every part of an area. • *Barefoot children roamed the streets.*

tissue /ˈtɪʃuː/, /ˈtɪsjuː/ NOUN In animals and plants, **tissue** consists of cells that are similar to each other in appearance and that have the same function. • *As we age we lose muscle tissue.*

TEST 1: READING

Passage 1

associate /əˈsəʊsieɪt/ (**associates, associating, associated**) VERB If one thing **is associated with** another thing, the two things are connected or related. • *These symptoms are associated with migraine headaches.*

beneficial /ˌbenɪˈfɪʃəl/ ADJECTIVE Something that is **beneficial** helps people or improves a situation. • *Using computers has a beneficial effect on children's learning.*

boost /buːst/ (boosts, boosting, boosted) VERB If one thing **boosts** another, it causes it to increase, improve or be more successful. • *Lower interest rates can boost the economy by reducing borrowing costs for consumers and businesses.*

diversity /daɪˈvɜːsɪti/, US /dɪ-/ NOUN The **diversity** of something is the fact that it contains many very different elements. • *...the cultural diversity of Latin America.*

dominate /ˈdɒmɪneɪt/ (dominates, dominating, dominated) VERB To **dominate** a situation or place means to be the most powerful or important person or thing in it. • *Their products dominate the global market for computer operating systems.*

efficiency /ɪˈfɪʃənsi/ NOUN **Efficiency** is the quality of being able to do something successfully, without wasting time or energy. • *There are many ways to increase agricultural efficiency in the poorer areas of the world.*

engage /ɪnˈɡeɪdʒ/ (engages, engaging, engaged) VERB [FORMAL] If you **engage in** or **are engaged in** an activity, you do it or are actively involved with it. • *Environmentalists are engaged in a battle to have jet skis banned from the bay.*

fertility /fɜːˈtɪlɪti/ NOUN **Fertility** is the ability of a plant to grow healthily in large numbers, or the ability of land to support the growth of a large number of strong healthy plants. • *He was able to bring large sterile acreages back to fertility.*

function /ˈfʌŋkʃən/ (functions) NOUN The **function** of something or someone is the useful thing that they do or are intended to do. • *This enzyme serves various functions.*

germinate /ˈdʒɜːmɪneɪt/ (germinates, germinating, germinated) VERB If a seed **germinates** or if it **is germinated**, it starts to grow. • *Some seed varieties germinate fast, so check every day or so.*

inhibit /ɪnˈhɪbɪt/ (inhibits, inhibiting, inhibited) VERB If something **inhibits** an event or process, it prevents it or slows it down. • *Excessive trace elements, such as copper, in the soil will inhibit plant growth.*

modification /mɒdɪfɪˈkeɪʃən/ NOUN **Modification** is the process of changing something slightly, usually in order to improve it. • *...behaviour modification techniques.*

mutual /ˈmjuːtʃuəl/ ADJECTIVE You use **mutual** to describe a situation, feeling or action that is experienced, felt or done by both of two people or things mentioned. • *The East and the West can work together for their mutual benefit.*

organism /ˈɔːɡənɪzəm/ (organisms) NOUN An **organism** is an animal or plant. • *Not all chemicals normally present in living organisms are harmless.*

promote /prəˈməʊt/ (promotes, promoting, promoted) VERB If people **promote** something, they help or encourage it to happen, increase or spread. • *You don't have to sacrifice environmental protection to promote economic growth.*

regulate /ˈreɡjʊleɪt/ (regulates, regulating, regulated) VERB To **regulate** an activity or process means to control it. • *...ways of regulating cholesterol levels.*

rot /rɒt/ (rots, rotting, rotted) VERB When food, wood or another substance **rots**, it becomes softer and is gradually destroyed. • *If we don't unload it soon, the grain will start rotting in the silos.*

soil /sɔɪl/ (soils) NOUN **Soil** is the substance on the surface of the earth in which plants grow. • *We have the most fertile soil in the county.*

stimulate /ˈstɪmjʊleɪt/ (stimulates, stimulating, stimulated) VERB To **stimulate** something means to encourage it to begin or develop further. • *America's priority is rightly to stimulate its economy.*

suppress /səˈpres/ (suppresses, suppressing, suppressed) VERB If someone or something **suppresses** a process or activity, they stop it continuing or developing. • *Diesel fumes have been shown to suppress immunity.*

sustainable /səˈsteɪnəbəl/ ADJECTIVE You use **sustainable** to describe the use of natural resources when this use is kept at a steady level that is not likely to damage the environment. • *...the management, conservation and sustainable development of forests.*

weed /wiːd/ (weeds) NOUN A **weed** is a wild plant that grows in gardens or fields of crops and prevents the plants that you want from growing properly. • *With repeated applications of weedkiller, the weeds were overcome.*

yield /jiːld/ (yields) NOUN A **yield** is the amount of food produced on an area of land or by a number of animals. • *...ways of improving the yield of the crop.*

Passage 2

accumulation /əkjuːmjʊˈleɪʃən/ NOUN **Accumulation** is the collecting together of things over a period of time. • *...the accumulation of capital.*

acquire /əˈkwaɪə/ (acquires, acquiring, acquired) VERB [FORMAL] If you **acquire** something, you buy or obtain it for yourself, or someone gives it to you. • *We have recently acquired a new painting.*

compulsion /kəmˈpʌlʃən/ (compulsions) NOUN A **compulsion** is a strong desire to do something, which you find difficult to control. • *He felt a sudden compulsion to drop the bucket and run.*

discard /dɪsˈkɑːd/ (discards, discarding, discarded) VERB If you **discard** something, you get rid of it because you no longer want it or need it. • *Read the manufacturer's guidelines before discarding the box.*

discipline /ˈdɪsɪplɪn/ (disciplines) NOUN [FORMAL] A **discipline** is a particular area of study, especially a subject of study in a college or university. • *We're looking for people from a wide range of disciplines.*

disorder /dɪsˈɔːdə/ (**disorders**) NOUN A **disorder** is a problem or illness which affects someone's mind or body. • *...a rare nerve disorder that can cause paralysis of the arms.*

evolutionary /iːvəˈluːʃənri/, US /-neri/ ADJECTIVE **Evolutionary** means relating to evolution, the process of gradual change over many generations by which species of animals, plants and insects develop. • *...an evolutionary process.*

sentimental /ˌsentɪˈmentəl/ ADJECTIVE **Sentimental** means relating to or involving feelings such as pity or love, especially for things in the past. • *Our paintings and photographs are of sentimental value only.*

trait /treɪt/, / treɪ/ (**traits**) NOUN A **trait** is a particular characteristic, quality or tendency that someone or something has. • *The study found that some alcoholics had clear personality traits showing up early in childhood.*

uninhabitable /ʌnɪnˈhæbɪtəbəl/ ADJECTIVE If a place is **uninhabitable**, it is impossible for people to live there, for example because it is dangerous or unhealthy. • *About 90 percent of the city's single-family homes are uninhabitable.*

Passage 3

account for /əˈkaʊnt fɔː/ (**accounts for, accounting for, accounted for**) PHRASAL VERB If a particular thing **accounts for** a part or proportion of something, that part or proportion consists of that thing. • *Computers account for 5% of the country's commercial electricity consumption.*

condition /kənˈdɪʃən/ (**conditions**) NOUN A **condition** is an illness or other medical problem. • *Doctors suspect he may have a heart condition.*

contract /kənˈtrækt/ (**contracts, contracting, contracted**) VERB [FORMAL] If you **contract** a serious illness, you become ill with it. • *He contracted AIDS from a blood transfusion.*

deterioration /dɪˌtɪəriəˈreɪʃən/ NOUN **Deterioriation** is the process of becoming worse. • *...the slow steady deterioration of a patient with Alzheimer's disease.*

hollow /ˈhɒləʊ/ ADJECTIVE Something that is **hollow** has a space inside it, as opposed to being solid all the way through. • *...a hollow tree.*

incurable /ɪnˈkjʊərəbəl/ ADJECTIVE If someone has an **incurable** disease, they cannot be cured of it. • *He is suffering from an incurable skin disease.*

inject /ɪnˈdʒekt/ (**injects, injecting, injected**) VERB To **inject** a substance such as a medicine into someone means to put it into their body using a device with a needle called a syringe. • *His son was injected with strong drugs.*

intensity /ɪnˈtensɪti/ NOUN The **intensity** of something is how great or extreme it is in strength or degree. • *...juices with a greater intensity of flavour.*

nutrient /ˈnjuːtriənt/, US /ˈnuː-/ (**nutrients**) NOUN **Nutrients** are substances that help plants and animals to grow. • *In her first book she explained the role of vegetable fibres, vitamins, minerals, and other essential nutrients.*

regain /rɪˈgeɪn/ (**regains, regaining, regained**) VERB If you **regain** something that you have lost, you get it back again. • *The experience helped me regain the confidence I lost when I failed my exams.*

register /ˈredʒɪstə/ (**registers, registering, registered**) VERB If you **register** as something or **register** to do something, you put your name on an official list, in order to be able to do something or to receive a service. • *Thousands lined up to register to vote.*

specialised /ˈspeʃəlaɪzd/ **specialized** ADJECTIVE Something that is **specialised** is developed especially for a particular purpose. • *Specialised equipment is available for working in particularly narrow spaces.*

stunning /ˈstʌnɪŋ/ ADJECTIVE If something is **stunning**, it is extremely unusual, unexpected or impressive. • *He resigned last night after a stunning defeat in Sunday's vote.*

transparent /trænsˈpærənt/, US /-ˈper-/ ADJECTIVE If an object or substance is **transparent**, you can see through it. • *...a sheet of transparent coloured plastic.*

vital /ˈvaɪtəl/ ADJECTIVE If you say that something is **vital**, you mean that it is necessary or very important. • *The port is vital to supply relief to millions of drought victims.*

TEST 2: LISTENING

Section 1

functional /ˈfʌŋkʃənəl/ ADJECTIVE **Functional** things are useful rather than decorative. • *...modern, functional furniture.*

restriction /rɪˈstrɪkʃən/ (**restrictions**) NOUN A **restriction** is an official rule that limits what you can do or that limits the amount or size of something. • *The relaxation of travel restrictions means they are free to travel and work.*

Section 2

assure /əˈʃʊə/ (**assures, assuring, assured**) VERB If you **assure** someone **that** something is true or will happen, you tell them that it is definitely true or will definitely happen, often in order to make them less worried. • *He hastened to assure me that there was nothing traumatic to report.*

petrified /ˈpetrɪfaɪd/ ADJECTIVE If you are **petrified**, you are extremely frightened, perhaps so frightened that you cannot think or move. • *I've always been petrified of being alone.*

swell up /swel ˈʌp/ (**swells up, swelling up, swelled up, swelled up, swollen up**) PHRASAL VERB If something such as a part of your body **swells up**, it becomes larger and rounder than normal. • *When you develop a throat infection or catch a cold the glands in the neck swell up.*

venom /'venəm/ NOUN The **venom** of a creature such as a snake or spider is the poison that it puts into your body when it bites or stings you. • *...snake handlers who grow immune to snake venom.*

Section 3

deadline /'dedlaɪn/ (**deadlines**) NOUN A **deadline** is a time or date before which a particular task must be finished or a particular thing must be done. • *We were not able to meet the deadline because of manufacturing delays.*

get into the swing of things /get ˌɪntu: ðə 'swɪŋ əv θɪŋz/ (**gets, getting, got**) [US] **gotten** PHRASE If you **get into the swing of things**, you become very involved with what you are doing and start to enjoy it. • *Everyone understood how hard it was to get back into the swing of things after such a long absence.*

overwhelming /ouvə'welmɪŋ/ ADJECTIVE If something is **overwhelming**, it affects you very strongly, and you do not know how to deal with it. • *The task won't feel so overwhelming if you break it down into small, easy-to-accomplish steps.*

Section 4

back at square one /bæk ət skweə 'wʌn/ PHRASE If you are **back at square one**, you have to start dealing with something from the beginning again because the way you were dealing with it has failed. • *If your complaint is not upheld, you may feel you are back at square one.*

donate /dəʊ'neɪt/ (**donates, donating, donated**) VERB If you **donate** something **to** a charity or other organisation, you give it to them. • *He frequently donates large sums to charity.*

emergence /ɪ'mɜːdʒəns/ NOUN The **emergence of** something is the process or event of its coming into existence. • *...the emergence of new democracies in Latin America.*

equity /'ekwɪti/ (**equities**) NOUN **Equities** are shares in a company that are owned by people who have a right to vote at the company's meetings and to receive part of the company's profits after the holders of preference shares have been paid. • *Investors have poured money into U.S. equities.*

factor in /fæktər 'ɪn/ (**factors in, factoring in, factored in**) PHRASAL VERB If you **factor in** a particular cost or element, you include it in a calculation. • *Using a computer model they factored in the costs of transplants for those women who die.*

funding /'fʌndɪŋ/ NOUN **Funding** is money which a government or organisation provides for a particular purpose. • *They hope for government funding for the scheme.*

initiative /ɪ'nɪʃətɪv/ (**initiatives**) NOUN An **initiative** is an action or plan that is intended to solve a problem. • *Local initiatives to help young people have been inadequate.*

margin /'mɑːdʒɪn/ (**margins**) NOUN A **margin** is the difference between two amounts, for example the amount you get by selling something and the amount you paid for it or the cost of making it. • *Fast-food chains tend to operate on low profit margins.*

monetary /'mʌnɪtri/, US /'mɑːnɪteri/ ADJECTIVE **Monetary** means relating to money. • *Various international monetary systems have been tried.*

pledge /pledʒ/ (**pledges**) NOUN When someone makes a **pledge**, they make a serious promise that they will do something. • *The meeting ended with a pledge to step up cooperation between the six states of the region.*

portal /'pɔːtəl/ (**portals**) NOUN On the Internet, a **portal** is a site that consists of links to other websites. • *...business-to-business portals which match buyers and sellers.*

potential See Test 1 Listening Section 3

return /rɪ'tɜːn/ (**returns**) NOUN The **return on** an investment is the profit that you get from it. • *Profits have picked up this year but the return on capital remains tiny.*

share /ʃeə/ (**shares**) NOUN A company's **shares** are the many equal parts into which its ownership is divided. Shares can be bought by people as an investment. • *People in China are eager to buy shares in new businesses.*

TEST 2: READING

Passage 1

absorb /əb'zɔːb/ (**absorbs, absorbing, absorbed**) VERB If something **absorbs** a liquid, gas or other substance, it soaks it up or takes it in. • *Plants absorb carbon dioxide from the air and moisture from the soil.*

aerial /'eəriəl/ ADJECTIVE An **aerial** photograph is one in which people or things on the ground are photographed from an aircraft. • *Patterns that are invisible on the ground can be the most striking part of an aerial photograph.*

beneficial See Test 1 Reading Passage 1

consume See Test 1 Listening Section 4

digest /daɪ'dʒest/ (**digests, digesting, digested**) VERB When you **digest** food, your body processes it and breaks it down so that the body can use the substances it needs and get rid of the rest. • *She couldn't digest food properly.*

edible /'edɪbəl/ ADJECTIVE If something is **edible**, it is safe to eat and not poisonous. • *...edible fungi.*

enable /ɪn'eɪbəl/ (**enables, enabling, enabled**) VERB If something **enables** a particular thing **to** happen, it makes it possible. • *The new test should enable doctors to detect the disease early.*

enormous /ɪˈnɔːməs/ ADJECTIVE Something that is **enormous** is extremely large in size or amount.
• *The main bedroom is enormous.*

evidence See Test 1 Listening Section 4

gigantic /dʒaɪˈɡæntɪk/ ADJECTIVE If you describe something as **gigantic**, you are emphasising that it is extremely large in size, amount, or degree.
• *In Red Rock Valley the road is bordered by gigantic rocks.*

nutrient See Test 1 Reading Passage 3

organism See Test 1 Reading Passage 1

poisonous /ˈpɔɪzənəs/ ADJECTIVE Something that is **poisonous** will kill you or make you ill if you swallow or absorb it. • *All parts of the yew tree are poisonous, including the berries.*

soil See Test 1 Reading Passage 1

stable /ˈsteɪbəl/ (stabler, stablest) ADJECTIVE
If something is **stable**, it is not likely to change or come to an end suddenly. • *The price of oil should remain stable for the rest of 1992.*

underground /ˌʌndəˈɡraʊnd/ ADVERB Something that happens **underground** happens below the surface of the ground. • *Solid low-level waste will be disposed of deep underground.*

Passage 2

adjust /əˈdʒʌst/ (adjusts, adjusting, adjusted) VERB
If you **adjust** something, you change it so that it is more effective or appropriate. • *Consider how you may need to adjust your behaviour when working in a foreign country.*

approval /əˈpruːvəl/ NOUN If someone or something has your **approval**, you like and admire them. • *His son had an obsessive drive to gain his father's approval.*

conscious /ˈkɒnʃəs/ ADJECTIVE If you are **conscious of** something, you notice it or realise that it is happening.
• *He was conscious of the faint, musky aroma of aftershave.*

crucial /ˈkruːʃəl/ ADJECTIVE If you describe something as **crucial**, you mean it is extremely important.
• *He had administrators under him but made the crucial decisions himself.*

dialect /ˈdaɪəlekt/ (dialects) NOUN A **dialect** is a form of a language that is spoken in a particular area.
• *It is often appropriate to use the local dialect to communicate your message.*

feature /ˈfiːtʃə/ (features) NOUN A **feature of** something is an interesting or important part or characteristic of it. • *The spacious gardens are a special feature of this property.*

indication /ˌɪndɪˈkeɪʃən/ (indications) NOUN
An **indication** is a sign that suggests or shows something, for example, what people are thinking or feeling. • *He gave no indication that he was ready to compromise.*

perceived /pəˈsiːvd/ ADJECTIVE A **perceived** difference, threat, risk, etc. is one that some people believe exists.
• *They have embraced the free market because of a perceived failure of the state.*

prestigious /preˈstɪdʒəs/ ADJECTIVE A **prestigious** institution, job or activity is respected and admired by people. • *It's one of the best equipped and most prestigious schools in the country.*

propose /prəˈpəʊz/ (proposes, proposing, proposed) VERB [FORMAL] If you **propose** a theory or an explanation, you state that it is possibly or probably true, because it fits in with the evidence that you have considered. • *This highlights a problem faced by people proposing theories of ball lightning.*

reveal /rɪˈviːl/ (reveals, revealing, revealed) VERB
To **reveal** something means to show it or tell people about it. • *She has refused to reveal the whereabouts of her daughter.*

status /ˈsteɪtəs/ NOUN **Status** is the importance and respect that someone has among the public or a particular group. • *Nurses are undervalued, and they never enjoy the same status as doctors.*

value /ˈvæljuː/ (values) NOUN The **values** of a person or group are the moral principles and beliefs that they think are important. • *The countries of South Asia also share many common values.*

version /ˈvɜːʃən/, / -ʒən/ (versions) NOUN
A **version** of something is a particular form of it in which some details are different from other forms.
• *Ludo is a version of an ancient Indian racing game.*

Passage 3

charge /tʃɑːdʒ/ (charges, charging, charged) VERB
If something **is charged** with electricity, an electrical current passes into it so that it carries an amount of electricity. • *A flash occurs when a gas is charged by an electrical spark.*

component /kəmˈpəʊnənt/ (components) NOUN
The **components** of something are the parts that it is made of. • *...automotive component suppliers to motor manufacturers.*

core /kɔː/ (cores) NOUN The **core** of an object, building or city is the central part of it. •*...the Earth's core.*

determine /dɪˈtɜːmɪn/ (determines, determining, determined) VERB [FORMAL] To **determine** a fact means to discover it as a result of investigation.
• *The investigation will determine what really happened.*

emission /ɪˈmɪʃən/ (emissions) NOUN [FORMAL]
An **emission of** something such as gas or radiation is the release of it into the atmosphere. • *Sulphur emissions from steel mills become acid rain.*

expose /ɪkˈspəʊz/ (exposes, exposing, exposed) VERB If something or someone **is exposed to** something dangerous or unpleasant, they are put in a situation in which it might affect them. • *...people exposed to high levels of radiation.*

fine /faɪn/ **(finer, finest)** ADJECTIVE A **fine** detail or distinction is very delicate, small or exact.
• *Johnson likes the broad outline but is reserving judgment on the fine detail.*

generate /'dʒenəreɪt/ **(generates, generating, generated)** VERB To **generate** a form of energy or power means to produce it. • *The company, New England Electric, burns coal to generate power.*

glow /gləʊ/ **(glows)** NOUN A **glow** is a dull, steady light, for example the light produced by a fire when there are no flames. • *The cigarette's red glow danced about in the darkness.*

intense /ɪn'tens/ ADJECTIVE **Intense** is used to describe something that is very great or extreme in strength or degree. • *He was sweating from the intense heat.*

intensify /ɪn'tensɪfaɪ/ **(intensifies, intensifying, intensified)** VERB If something **intensifies**, it becomes greater in strength, amount or degree. • *The conflict is almost bound to intensify.*

magnetic field /mægˌnetɪk 'fiːld/ **(magnetic fields)** NOUN A **magnetic field** is an area around a magnet, or something functioning as a magnet, in which the magnet's power to attract things is felt.
• *Earth is a huge magnet and possesses its own magnetic field.*

orbit /'ɔːbɪt/ **(orbits)** NOUN An **orbit** is the curved path in space that is followed by an object going around and around a planet, moon or star. • *Mars and Earth have orbits which change with time.*

particle /'pɑːtɪkəl/ **(particles)** NOUN In physics, a **particle** is a piece of matter smaller than an atom, such as an electron or a proton. • *...the subatomic particles that make up matter.*

province /'prɒvɪns/ **(provinces)** NOUN A **province** is a large section of a country that has its own administration. • *...the Algarve, Portugal's southernmost province.*

satellite /'sætəlaɪt/ **(satellites)** NOUN A **satellite** is an object which has been sent into space in order to collect information or to be part of a communications system. Satellites move continually around the earth or around another planet. • *The rocket launched two communications satellites.*

sensor /'sensə/ **(sensors)** NOUN A **sensor** is an instrument which reacts to certain physical conditions or impressions such as heat or light, and which is used to provide information. • *The latest Japanese vacuum cleaners contain sensors that detect the amount of dust and type of floor.*

subatomic /ˌsʌbə'tɒmɪk/ ADJECTIVE A **subatomic** particle is a particle which is part of an atom, for example an electron, a proton or a neutron.
• *...the subatomic particles that make up matter.*

surge /sɜːdʒ/ **(surges)** NOUN A **surge** is a sudden large increase in a physical force such as wind or electricity.
• *The whole car shuddered with an almost frightening surge of power.*

trigger /'trɪgə/ **(triggers, triggering, triggered)** VERB If something **triggers** an event or situation, it causes it to begin to happen or exist. • *...the incident which triggered the outbreak of the First World War.*

TEST 3: LISTENING

Section 1

claim /kleɪm/ **(claims, claiming, claimed)** VERB If you **claim** money from an insurance company or another organisation, you officially apply to them for it, because you think you are entitled to it according to their rules.
• *John had taken out insurance but when he tried to claim, the insurance company refused to pay.*

cover /'kʌvə/ **(covers)** Insurance **cover** is a guarantee from an insurance company that money will be paid by them if it is needed. • *Make sure that the firm's insurance cover is adequate.*

extraction /ɪk'strækʃən/ **(extractions)** NOUN The **extraction** of a tooth is the act of removing it from a person's mouth. • *In those days, dentistry was basic. Extractions were carried out without anaesthetic.*

slot /slɒt/ **(slots)** NOUN A **slot** in a schedule or programme is a time in it where an activity can take place. • *Visitors can book a time slot a week or more in advance.*

Section 2

beneficial See Test 1 Reading Passage 1

frame of mind /freɪm əv 'maɪnd/ **(frames of mind)** NOUN Your **frame of mind** is the mood that you are in, which causes you to have a particular attitude to something. • *Lewis was not in the right frame of mind to continue.*

insight /'ɪnsaɪt/ **(insights)** NOUN If you gain **insight** or an **insight into** a situation or problem, you gain an accurate understanding of it. • *The project would give scientists new insights into what is happening to the Earth's atmosphere.*

knit /nɪt/ **(knits, knitting, knitted)** VERB If you **knit** something, especially an article of clothing, you make it from wool or a similar thread by using two knitting needles or a machine. • *I had endless hours to knit and sew.*

print /prɪnt/ **(prints)** NOUN A **print** is one of a number of copies of a particular picture. It can be either a photograph, something such as a painting, or a picture made by an artist who puts ink on a prepared surface and presses it against paper. • *...12 original copper plates engraved by William Hogarth for his famous series of prints.*

rekindle /ˌriː'kɪndəl/ **(rekindles, rekindling, rekindled)** VERB If something **rekindles** an interest, feeling or thought that you used to have, it makes you think about it or feel it again. • *Her interest was rekindled when she saw herbs in everyday medicinal use there.*

writer's block /ˌraɪtəz ˈblɒk/ NOUN If you suffer from **writer's block**, you are unable to think of any new ideas for your writing, or to decide how to write about something. • *I find that swimming is a good cure for writer's block.*

Section 3

flexible /ˈfleksɪbəl/ ADJECTIVE Something or someone that is **flexible** is able or willing to change and adapt to different circumstances. • *...flexible working hours.*

funding /ˈfʌndɪŋ/ NOUN **Funding** is money which a government or organisation provides for a particular purpose. • *Many colleges have seen their funding cut.*

pick someone's brains /ˌpɪk ˈbreɪnz/ PHRASE If you **pick** someone's **brains**, you ask them to help you with a problem because they know more about the subject than you. • *Why should a successful company allow another firm to pick its brains?*

restriction See Test 2 Listening Section 1

Section 4

associate See Test 1 Reading Passage 1

condition See Test 1 Reading Passage 3

consistently /kənˈsɪstəntli/ ADVERB If someone does something **consistently**, they always do it in the same way. • *It's something I have consistently denied.*

evidence See Test 1 Listening Section 4

infant /ˈɪnfənt/ (infants) NOUN [FORMAL] An **infant** is a baby or very young child. • *...vaccinations of newborn infants.*

intrinsic /ɪnˈtrɪnsɪk/ ADJECTIVE [FORMAL] If something has **intrinsic** value or **intrinsic** interest, it is valuable or interesting because of its basic nature or character, and not because of its connection with other things. • *Diamonds have little intrinsic value and their price depends almost entirely on their scarcity.*

prevalent /ˈprevələnt/ ADJECTIVE A condition, practice, or belief that is **prevalent** is common. • *This condition is more prevalent in women than in men.*

spatially /ˈspeɪʃəli/ ADVERB **Spatially** means in a way that relates to shapes, spaces and areas. • *We conceive of time spatially, as a line going back and forwards.*

stimulate /ˈstɪmjʊleɪt/ (stimulates, stimulating, stimulated) VERB If something **stimulates** a part of a person's body, it causes it to move or start working. • *Exercise stimulates the digestive and excretory systems.*

subjective /səbˈdʒektɪv/ ADJECTIVE Something that is **subjective** is based on personal opinions and feelings rather than on facts. • *The way they interpreted their past was highly subjective.*

TEST 3: READING

Passage 1

associate See Test 1 Reading Passage 1

cognitive /ˈkɒɡnɪtɪv/ ADJECTIVE [FORMAL] **Cognitive** means relating to the mental process involved in knowing, learning and understanding things. • *As children grow older, their cognitive processes become sharper.*

condition /kənˈdɪʃən/ (conditions) NOUN A **condition** is an illness or other medical problem. • *Doctors suspect he may have a heart condition.*

critical /ˈkrɪtɪkəl/ ADJECTIVE A **critical** time, factor or situation is extremely important. • *The incident happened at a critical point in the campaign.*

disorder /dɪsˈɔːdə/ (disorders) NOUN A **disorder** is a problem or illness which affects someone's mind or body. • *...a rare nerve disorder that can cause paralysis of the arms.*

element /ˈelɪmənt/ (elements) NOUN The different **elements** of something are the different parts it contains. • *The plot has all the elements not only of romance but of high drama.*

equivalent /ɪˈkwɪvələnt/ ADJECTIVE If something is **equivalent** to something else, it has the same value or function in a different time, place or system • *...a decrease of 10% in property investment compared with the equivalent period in 1991.*

fragile /ˈfrædʒaɪl/, US /-dʒəl/ ADJECTIVE Something that is **fragile** is weak or easily broken. • *He leaned back in his fragile chair.*

function See Test 1 Reading Passage 1

hug /hʌɡ/ (hugs, hugging, hugged) VERB When you **hug** someone, you put your arms around them and hold them tightly, for example because you like them or are pleased to see them. • *She had hugged him exuberantly and invited him to dinner the next day.*

infancy /ˈɪnfənsi/ NOUN **Infancy** is the period of your life when you are a very young child. • *...the development of the mind from infancy onwards.*

intervention /ˌɪntəˈvenʃən/ NOUN **Intervention** is the act of becoming involved in a situation and trying to change it. • *She seemed to have got better with no treatment or medical intervention.*

mutation /mjuːˈteɪʃən/ (mutations) NOUN A **mutation** is a change in a gene that causes a plant or animal to develop different characteristics. • *Scientists have found a genetic mutation that appears to be the cause of Huntington's disease.*

operation /ˌɒpəˈreɪʃən/ (operations) NOUN When a patient has an **operation**, a surgeon cuts open their body in order to remove, replace, or repair a diseased or damaged part. • *Charles was in hospital recovering from an operation on his arm.*

pregnancy /'pregnənsi/ NOUN **Pregnancy** is the condition of having a baby developing in your body. • *It would be wiser to cut out all alcohol during pregnancy.*

reject /rɪ'dʒekt/ (rejects, rejecting, rejected) VERB If someone **rejects** another person or **rejects** their affection, they are cold and unfriendly towards them. • *...people who had been rejected by their families.*

tactile /'tæktaɪl/, US /-təl/ ADJECTIVE **Tactile** means relating to the sense of touch or to experiences that are received by touch. • *Babies who sleep with their parents receive much more tactile stimulation than babies who sleep in a cot.*

transparent See Test 1 Reading Passage 3

treatment /'triːtmənt/ NOUN **Treatment** is medical attention given to a sick or injured person. • *Many patients are not getting the medical treatment they need.*

withdrawal /wɪð'drɔːəl/ NOUN **Withdrawal** is behaviour in which someone prefers to be alone and does not want to talk to other people. • *...an inability to cope with emotional problems except by retreating into withdrawal.*

womb /wuːm/ (wombs) NOUN A woman's **womb** is the part inside her body where a baby grows before it is born. • *Some people claim they can remember being in the womb.*

Passage 2

bacteria /bæk'tɪəriə/ NOUN **Bacteria** are very small organisms. Some bacteria can cause disease. • *Chlorine is added to kill bacteria.*

capable /'keɪpəbəl/ ADJECTIVE If a person or thing is **capable of** doing something, they have the ability to do it. • *The kitchen is capable of catering for several hundred people.*

circulation /sɜːkjʊ'leɪʃən/ NOUN The **circulation** of something within a closed place or system is its free and easy movement within the place or system. • *The north pole is warmer than the south and the circulation of air around it is less well contained.*

construction /kən'strʌkʃən/ NOUN You use **construction** to refer to the structure of something and the way it has been built or made. • *The Shakers believed that furniture should be plain, simple, useful, practical and of sound construction.*

decomposition /diːkɒmpə'zɪʃən/ NOUN **Decomposition** is the process of decay that takes place when a living thing changes chemically after dying. [FORMAL] • *The decomposition of dead organisms in soil releases minerals which can be reused by other living organisms.*

digestive system /daɪ'dʒestɪv ˌsɪstəm/ (digestive systems) NOUN Your **digestive system** is the system in your body that digests the food you eat. • *The digestive system has to cope with the various stages of breaking down food.*

disposal /dɪs'pəʊzəl/ NOUN **Disposal** is the act of getting rid of something that is no longer wanted or needed. • *...methods for the permanent disposal of radioactive wastes.*

distribute /dɪ'strɪbjuːt/ (distributes, distributing, distributed) VERB If you **distribute** things, you give them or deliver them to a number of people. • *Profits are distributed among the policyholders.*

dominate /'dɒmɪneɪt/ (dominates, dominating, dominated) VERB To **dominate** a situation or place means to be the most powerful or important person or thing in it. • *Their products dominate the global market for computer operating systems.*

ensure /ɪn'ʃʊə/ (ensures, ensuring, ensured) VERB To **ensure** something, or to **ensure that** something happens, means to make certain that it happens. [FORMAL] • *We must ensure that all patients have access to high quality care.*

extend /ɪk'stend/ (extends, extending, extended) VERB If an object **extends from** a surface or place, it sticks out from it. • *A table extended from the front of her desk to create a T-shaped seating arrangement.*

harvest /'hɑːvɪst/ (harvests, harvesting, harvested) VERB When you **harvest** a crop, you gather it in. • *Rice farmers here still plant and harvest their crops by hand.*

instrumental /ˌɪnstrə'mentəl/ ADJECTIVE Someone or something that is **instrumental in** a process or event helps to make it happen. • *In his first years as chairman he was instrumental in raising the company's wider profile.*

mutual See Test 1 Reading Passage 1

parasitise also **parasitize** /'pærəsɪˌtaɪz, 'pærəsaɪˌtaɪz/ (parasitises, parasitising, parasitised) VERB If an animal or plant **parasitises** another animal or plant, it lives on it or inside it and gets its food from it. • *One type of wasp parasitises caterpillars of butterflies and moths.*

pollinate /'pɒlɪneɪt/ (pollinates, pollinating, pollinated) VERB To **pollinate** a plant or tree means to fertilise it with pollen. This is often done by insects. • *Many of the indigenous insects are needed to pollinate the local plants.*

reaction /ri'ækʃən/ (reactions) NOUN A **reaction to** something that happens or to something that you touch is what you do because of it, or how you are affected by it. • *Every year, 5,000 people have life-threatening reactions to anaesthetics.*

sophistication /səˌfɪstɪ'keɪʃən/ NOUN The **sophistication** of people, places, machines or methods is their quality of being more advanced or complex than others. • *...the technological sophistication of modern weaponry.*

suffocation /ˌsʌfə'keɪʃən/ NOUN **Suffocation** is the process of dying because there is no air to breathe. • *Many of the victims died of suffocation.*

supplement /ˈsʌplɪmənt/ (supplements, supplementing, supplemented) VERB If you **supplement** something, you add something to it in order to improve it. • *I suggest supplementing your diet with vitamins E and A.*

toxic /ˈtɒksɪk/ ADJECTIVE A **toxic** substance is poisonous. • *These products are not toxic to humans.*

unique /juːˈniːk/ ADJECTIVE If something is **unique to** one thing, person, group or place, it concerns or belongs only to that thing, person, group or place. • *No one knows for sure why adolescence is unique to humans.*

Passage 3

adulthood /ˈædʌlthʊd/, US /əˈdʌlt-/ NOUN **Adulthood** is the state of being an adult. • *Most people catch the illness before they reach adulthood.*

associate See Test 1 Reading Passage 1

conversely /ˈkɒnvɜːsli /, /kənˈvɜːsli/ ADVERB You say **conversely** to indicate that the situation you are about to describe is the opposite or reverse of the one you have just described. [FORMAL] • *That makes Chinese products even cheaper and, conversely, makes American-made goods more expensive to export.*

decline /dɪˈklaɪn/ (declines, declining, declined) VERB If something **declines**, it becomes less in quantity, importance or strength. • *Hourly output by workers declined 1.3% in the first quarter.*

degenerate /dɪˈdʒenəreɪt/ (degenerates, degenerating, degenerated) VERB If you say that someone or something **degenerates**, you mean that they become worse in some way, for example, weaker, lower in quality or more dangerous. • *Inactivity can make your joints stiff, and the bones may begin to degenerate.*

discard See Test 1 Reading Passage 2

efficiency See Test 1 Reading Passage 1

experimental /ɪkˌsperɪˈmentəl/ ADJECTIVE **Experimental** means using, used in, or resulting from scientific experiments. • *We have experimental and observational evidence concerning things which happened before and after the origin of life.*

intensive /ɪnˈtensɪv/ ADJECTIVE **Intensive** activity involves concentrating a lot of effort or people on one particular task in order to try to achieve a lot in a short time. • *...after several days and nights of intensive negotiations.*

landmark /ˈlændmɑːk/ (landmarks) NOUN You can refer to an important stage in the development of something as a **landmark**. • *In a landmark decision, the council of the Law Society voted to dismantle its present governing body.*

massively /ˈmæsɪvli/ ADVERB **Massively** means very or very much. • *...a massively popular game.*

profound /prəˈfaʊnd/ (profounder, profoundest) ADJECTIVE You use **profound** to emphasise that something is very great or intense. • *...discoveries which had a profound effect on many areas of medicine.*

refute /rɪˈfjuːt/ (refutes, refuting, refuted) VERB If you **refute** an argument, accusation or theory, you prove that it is wrong or untrue. [FORMAL] • *It was the kind of rumour that it is impossible to refute.*

regenerate /rɪˈdʒenəreɪt/ (regenerates, regenerating, regenerated) VERB If organs or tissues **regenerate** or if something **regenerates** them, they heal and grow again after they have been damaged. • *Nerve cells have limited ability to regenerate if destroyed.*

region /ˈriːdʒən/ (regions) NOUN You can refer to a part of your body as a **region**. • *...the pelvic region.*

reside /rɪˈzaɪd/ (resides, residing, resided) VERB If someone or something **resides** somewhere, they live there or are found there. [FORMAL] • *Candida bacteria reside in the digestive system.*

spot /spɒt/ (spots) NOUN You can refer to a particular place as a **spot**. • *They stayed at several of the island's top tourist spots.*

stable See Test 2 Reading Passage 1

tissue See Test 1 Listening Section 4

TEST 4: LISTENING

Section 1

concussion /kənˈkʌʃən/ NOUN If you suffer **concussion** after a blow to your head, you lose consciousness or feel sick or confused. • *Nicky was rushed to hospital with concussion.*

junction /ˈdʒʌŋkʃən/ (junctions) NOUN A **junction** is a place where roads or railway lines join. [BRIT] • *At the junction there was a queue of traffic on the main road.*

pull out /pʊl ˈaʊt/ (pulls out, pulling out, pulled out) PHRASAL VERB When a vehicle or driver **pulls out**, the vehicle moves out into the road or nearer the centre of the road. • *She started up the engine, and pulled out into the road.*

Section 2

defrost /diːˈfrɒst/, US /-ˈfrɔːst/ (defrosts, defrosting, defrosted) VERB When you **defrost** a fridge or freezer, you switch it off or press a special switch so that the ice inside it can melt. You can also say that a fridge or freezer **is defrosting**. • *Defrost the fridge regularly so that it works at maximum efficiency.*

draught /drɑːft/, /dræft/ (draughts) NOUN A **draught** is a current of air that comes into a place in an undesirable way. • *Block draughts around doors and windows.*

insulate /'ɪnsjʊˌleɪt/, us /-sə-/ **(insulates, insulating, insulated)** VERB To **insulate** something such as a building means to protect it from cold or noise by covering it or surrounding it in a thick layer. • *It will take almost 25 years to insulate the homes of the six million households that require this assistance.*

laundry /'lɔːndri/ NOUN **Laundry** is used to refer to clothes, sheets and towels that are about to be washed, are being washed or have just been washed. • *I'll do your laundry.*

radiator /'reɪdiˌeɪtə/ **(radiators)** NOUN A **radiator** is a hollow metal device, usually connected by pipes to a central heating system, that is used to heat a room. • *There were clothes drying on the radiator.*

Section 3

accountancy /ə'kaʊntənsi/ NOUN **Accountancy** is the theory or practice of keeping financial accounts. • *He's sitting his final exams in accountancy.*

tag along /ˌtæg ə'lɒŋ/ **(tags along, tagging along, tagged along)** PHRASAL VERB If someone goes somewhere and you **tag along**, you go with them, especially when they have not asked you to. • *She seems quite happy to tag along with them.*

Section 4

breeding ground /'briːdɪŋ ˌgraʊnd/ **(breeding grounds)** NOUN The **breeding ground for** a particular type of creature is the place where this creature breeds easily. • *The swamp is a perfect breeding ground for malarial mosquitoes.*

conservation /ˌkɒnsə'veɪʃən/ NOUN **Conservation** is saving and protecting the environment. • *...a four-nation regional meeting on elephant conservation.*

enable See Test 2 Reading Passage 1

expanse /ɪk'spæns/ **(expanses)** NOUN An **expanse of** something, usually sea, sky or land, is a very large amount of it. • *...a vast expanse of grassland.*

hypothesise /haɪ'pɒθɪˌsaɪz/ **(hypothesises, hypothesising, hypothesised, hypothesize)** VERB If you **hypothesise that** something will happen, you say that you think that thing will happen because of various facts you have considered. [FORMAL] • *To explain this, they hypothesise that galaxies must contain a great deal of missing matter which cannot be detected.*

map /mæp/ **(maps, mapping, mapped)** VERB To **map** something means to discover and record its position, where it moves or how it is organised. • *The ambitious project will seek to map the movement of humans across the globe.*

migratory /'maɪgrətəri/, us /-tɔːri/ ADJECTIVE **Migratory** means relating to the migration of people, birds, fish or animals. • *Salmon are migratory fish with a remarkable life cycle.*

monitor /'mɒnɪtə/ **(monitors, monitoring, monitored)** VERB If you **monitor** something, you regularly check its development or progress, and sometimes comment on it. • *Senior managers can then use the budget as a control document to monitor progress against the agreed actions.*

plot /plɒt/ **(plots, plotting, plotted)** VERB If someone **plots** the progress or development of something, they make a diagram or a plan which shows how it has developed in order to give some indication of how it will develop in the future. • *They used a computer to plot the movements of everyone in the police station on December 24, 2010.*

utilise /'juːtɪˌlaɪz/ **(utilises, utilising, utilised)** **utilize** VERB If you **utilise** something, you use it. [FORMAL] • *Sound engineers utilise a range of techniques to enhance the quality of the recordings.*

TEST 4: READING

Passage 1

accelerate /æk'seləreɪt/ **(accelerates, accelerating, accelerated)** VERB When a moving vehicle or object **accelerates**, or when something **accelerates** it, it goes faster and faster. • *Its 191kW engine accelerates it from 0 to 100km / h in about 9.5 seconds.*

altitude /'æltɪtjuːd/, us /-tuːd/ **(altitudes)** NOUN If something is at a particular **altitude**, it is at that height above sea level. • *The aircraft had reached its cruising altitude of about 39,000 feet.*

core See Test 2 Reading Passage 3

dawn /dɔːn/ NOUN **Dawn** is the time of day when light first appears in the sky, just before the sun rises. • *Nancy woke at dawn.*

dense /dens/ **(denser, densest)** ADJECTIVE A **dense** substance is very heavy in relation to its volume. • *The densest ocean water is the coldest and most saline.*

diameter /daɪ'æmɪtə/ **(diameters)** NOUN The **diameter** of a round object is the length of a straight line that can be drawn across it, passing through the middle of it. • *...a length of 22-mm diameter steel pipe.*

encounter /ɪn'kaʊntə/ **(encounters, encountering, encountered)** VERB To **encounter** someone or something is to meet, discover or experience them, usually unexpectedly. [FORMAL] • *Did you encounter anyone in the building?*

fracture /'fræktʃə/ **(fractures, fracturing, fractured)** VERB If something **is fractured** or **fractures**, it gets a crack or break in it. • *One strut had fractured and been crudely repaired in several places.*

fragment /'frægmənt/ **(fragments)** NOUN A **fragment of** something is a small piece or part of it. • *The only reminder of the shooting is a few fragments of metal in my shoulder.*

originate /əˈrɪdʒɪneɪt/ (originates, originating, originated) VERB When something **originates** or when someone **originates** it, it begins to happen or exist. [FORMAL] • *All carbohydrates originate from plants.*

phase /feɪz/ (phases) NOUN A **phase** is a particular stage in a process or in the gradual development of something. • *This autumn, 6,000 residents will participate in the first phase of the project.*

resistance /rɪˈzɪstəns/ NOUN Wind or air **resistance** is a force which slows down a moving object or vehicle. • *The design of the bicycle reduces the effects of wind resistance and drag.*

scarce /skeəs/ (scarcer, scarcest) ADJECTIVE If something is **scarce**, there is not enough of it. • *Jobs are becoming increasingly scarce.*

shockwave /ˈʃɒkweɪv/ (shockwaves) NOUN A **shockwave** is an area of very high pressure moving through the air, earth or water. It is caused by an explosion or an earthquake, or by an object travelling faster than sound. • *The shockwaves yesterday were felt from Las Vegas to San Diego.*

split /splɪt/ (splits, splitting, split) VERB If something **splits** or if you **split** it, it is divided into two or more parts. • *In a severe gale the ship split in two.*

strike /straɪk/ (strikes) NOUN A **strike** is an occasion when something that is falling or moving hits something else. • *...climatic change caused by a huge meteor strike.*

vaporise /ˈveɪpəraɪz/ (vaporises, vaporising, vaporised) **vaporize** VERB If a liquid or solid **vaporises** or if you **vaporise** it, it changes into vapour or gas. • *The benzene vaporised and formed a huge cloud of gas.*

vital See Test 1 Reading Passage 3

Passage 2

aluminium /ˌæluˈmɪniəm/ NOUN **Aluminium** is a lightweight metal used, for example, for making cooking equipment and aircraft parts. • *aluminium cans*

bury /ˈberi/ (buries, burying, buried) VERB To **bury** something means to put it into a hole in the ground and cover it up with earth. • *They make the charcoal by burying wood in the ground and then slowly burning it.*

coherent /kəʊˈhɪərənt/ ADJECTIVE If something is **coherent**, it is well planned, so that it is clear and sensible and all its parts go well with each other. • *He has failed to work out a coherent strategy for modernising the service.*

concept /ˈkɒnsept/ (concepts) NOUN A **concept** is an idea or abstract principle. • *...basic legal concepts.*

considerable /kənˈsɪdərəbəl/ ADJECTIVE **Considerable** means great in amount or degree. [FORMAL] • *Other studies found considerable evidence to support this finding.*

controversial /ˌkɒntrəˈvɜːʃəl/ ADJECTIVE If you describe something or someone as **controversial**, you mean that they are the subject of intense public argument, disagreement or disapproval. • *Immigration is a controversial issue in many countries.*

diligently /ˈdɪlɪdʒəntli/ ADVERB If you do something **diligently**, you do it in a careful and thorough way. • *The two sides are now working diligently to resolve their differences.*

disposal See Test 3 Reading Passage 2

distribute /dɪˈstrɪbjuːt/ (distributes, distributing, distributed) VERB If you **distribute** things, you hand them or deliver them to a number of people. • *Profits are distributed among the policyholders.*

efficiency See Test 1 Reading Passage 1

fine /faɪn/ (fines, fining, fined) VERB If someone **is fined**, they are punished by being ordered to pay a sum of money because they have done something illegal or broken a rule. • *An East London school has set a precedent by fining pupils who break the rules.*

foil /fɔɪl/ NOUN **Foil** consists of sheets of metal as thin as paper. It is used to wrap food in. • *Pour cider around the meat and cover with foil.*

generate See Test 2 Reading Passage 3

incineration /ɪnˌsɪnəˈreɪʃən/ NOUN **Incineration** is the process of burning rubbish or waste material completely in a special container. • *...banning the incineration of lead batteries.*

initiative See Test 2 Listening Section 4

labourer /ˈleɪbərə/ (labourers) NOUN A **labourer** is a person who does a job which involves a lot of hard physical work. • *She still lives on the farm where he worked as a labourer.*

range /reɪndʒ/ (ranges) NOUN A **range of** things is a number of different things of the same general kind. • *The two men discussed a range of issues.*

scheme /skiːm/ (schemes) NOUN A **scheme** is a plan or arrangement involving many people which is made by a government or other organisation. [BRIT] • *...schemes to help combat unemployment.*

scrap metal /skræp ˈmetəl/ NOUN **Scrap metal** is metal from old or damaged machinery or cars. • *They crush the cars for scrap metal.*

sense /sens/ NOUN If a course of action **makes sense**, it seems sensible. • *The project should be re-appraised to see whether it made sound economic sense.*

strategy /ˈstrætədʒi/ (strategies) NOUN A **strategy** is a general plan or set of plans intended to achieve something, especially over a long period. • *Next week, health ministers gather in Amsterdam to agree a strategy for controlling malaria.*

Passage 3

advent /'ædvent/ NOUN **The advent of** an important event, invention or situation is the fact of it starting or coming into existence. [FORMAL] • *The advent of the computer has brought this sort of task within the bounds of possibility.*

advocate /'ædvəkət/ **(advocates)** NOUN An **advocate of** a particular action or plan is someone who recommends it publicly. [FORMAL] • *He was a strong advocate of free market policies and a multi-party system.*

aggregate /'ægrɪɡeɪt/ **(aggregates, aggregating, aggregated)** VERB If amounts or things **are aggregated**, they are added together and considered as a single amount or thing. [FORMAL] • *We should never aggregate votes to predict results under another system.*

allocate /'æləkeɪt/ **(allocates, allocating, allocated)** VERB If one item or share of something **is allocated to** a particular person or **for** a particular purpose, it is given to that person or used for that purpose. • *The 1985 federal budget allocated $7.3 billion for development programmes.*

brutal /'bruːtəl/ ADJECTIVE **Brutal** is used to describe things that have an unpleasant effect on people, especially when there is no attempt by anyone to reduce their effect. • *The dip in prices this summer will be brutal.*

commercial /kə'mɜːʃəl/ ADJECTIVE **Commercial** organisations and activities are concerned with making money or profits, rather than, for example, with scientific research or providing a public service. • *Whether the project will be a commercial success is still uncertain.*

commitment /kə'mɪtmənt/ NOUN **Commitment** is a strong belief in an idea or system. • *...commitment to the ideals of democracy.*

commodity /kə'mɒdɪti/ **(commodities)** NOUN A **commodity** is something that is sold for money. • *Unlike gold, most commodities are not kept solely for investment purposes.*

component See Test 2 Reading Passage 3

consumption /kən'sʌmpʃən/ NOUN **Consumption** is the act of buying and using things. • *...the production and consumption of goods and services.*

contract /'kɒntrækt/ **(contracts)** NOUN A **contract** is a legal agreement, usually between two companies or between an employer and employee, which involves doing work for a stated sum of money. • *The company won a hefty contract for work on Chicago's tallest building.*

conventional /kən'venʃənəl/ ADJECTIVE A **conventional** method or product is one that is usually used or that has been in use for a long time. • *Conventional methods of producing power also carry some safety risks.*

daunting /'dɔːntɪŋ/ ADJECTIVE Something that is **daunting** makes you feel slightly afraid or worried about dealing with it. • *...the daunting task of restoring the gardens to their former splendour.*

device /dɪ'vaɪs/ **(devices)** NOUN A **device** is an object that has been invented for a particular purpose, for example, for recording or measuring something. • *...the electronic device that tells the starter when an athlete has moved from his blocks prematurely.*

disrupt /dɪs'rʌpt/ **(disrupts, disrupting, disrupted)** VERB If someone or something **disrupts** an event, system or process, they cause difficulties that prevent it from continuing or operating in a normal way. • *The drought has severely disrupted agricultural production.*

distinguished /dɪ'stɪŋɡwɪʃt/ ADJECTIVE If you describe a person or their work as **distinguished**, you mean that they have been very successful in their career and have a good reputation. • *His distinguished works on labour history will be familiar to readers.*

domestic /də'mestɪk/ ADJECTIVE **Domestic** political activities, events and situations happen or exist within one particular country. • *...sales in the domestic market.*

elimination /ɪˌlɪmɪ'neɪʃən/ NOUN The **elimination** of something is its complete removal. [FORMAL] • *...the prohibition and elimination of chemical weapons.*

estate /ɪ'steɪt/ **(estates)** NOUN An **estate** is a large area of land in the country which is owned by a person, family or organisation. • *He spent holidays at the 300-acre estate of his aunt and uncle.*

fleet /fliːt/ **(fleets)** NOUN A **fleet** of vehicles is a group of them, especially when they all belong to a particular organisation or business, or when they are all going somewhere together. • *With its own fleet of trucks, the company delivers most orders overnight.*

flexible See Test 3 Listening Section 3

fundamentally /ˌfʌndə'mentəli/ ADVERB You use **fundamentally** to indicate that something affects or relates to the deep, basic nature of something. • *Environmentalists say the treaty is fundamentally flawed.*

grab /græb/ **(grabs, grabbing, grabbed)** VERB If you **grab** something, you take it or pick it up suddenly or eagerly. • *She grabbed the chance of a job interview.*

haunt /hɔːnt/ **(haunts, haunting, haunted)** VERB If something unpleasant **haunts** you, you keep thinking or worrying about it over a long period of time. • *There is no spectre of fascism haunting Europe.*

impact /'ɪmpækt/ **(impacts)** NOUN The **impact** that something has **on** a situation, process or person is a sudden and powerful effect that it has on them. • *...an area where technology can make a real impact.*

implication /ˌɪmplɪ'keɪʃən/ **(implications)** NOUN **The implications of** something are the things that are likely to happen as a result. • *The low level of investment has serious implications for future economic growth.*

inclined /ɪnˈklaɪnd/ ADJECTIVE If you are **inclined to** behave in a particular way, you often behave in that way, or you want to do so. • *If you are so inclined, you can watch TV.*

liability /ˌlaɪəˈbɪlɪti/ (liabilities) NOUN If you say that someone or something is **a liability**, you mean that they cause a lot of problems or embarrassment. • *The party's traditional strengths have become liabilities.*

liquid /ˈlɪkwɪd/ NOUN A **liquid** is a substance which is not solid but which flows and can be poured, for example water. • *Solids turn to liquids at certain temperatures.*

mature /məˈtjʊə/ (maturer, maturest) ADJECTIVE If you describe an economy, industry or market as **mature**, you think that it is fully developed and advanced and does not need further investment or expansion • *Many investors put money into mature industries to balance riskier investments in newer businesses.*

middleman /ˈmɪdəlˌmæn/ (middlemen) NOUN A **middleman** is a person or company which buys things from the people who produce them and sells them to the people who want to buy them. • *Why don't they cut out the middleman and let us do it ourselves?*

niche /niːʃ/, US /nɪtʃ/ (niches) NOUN A **niche** in the market is a specific area of marketing which has its own particular requirements, customers and products. • *Small companies can do extremely well if they can fill a specific market niche.*

ominous /ˈɒmɪnəs/ ADJECTIVE If you describe something as **ominous**, you mean that it worries you because it makes you think that something bad is going to happen. • *There was an ominous silence at the other end of the phone.*

outsource /aʊtˈsɔːs/ (outsources, outsourcing, outsourced) VERB If a company **outsources** work or things, it pays workers from outside the company to do the work or supply the things. • *Increasingly, corporate clients are seeking to outsource the management of their facilities.*

prototype /ˈprəʊtəˌtaɪp/ (prototypes) NOUN A **prototype** is a new type of machine or device that is not yet ready to be made in large numbers and sold. • *...the first prototype aircraft.*

radically /ˈrædɪkli/ ADVERB If something changes **radically**, it changes completely, in a very important way. • *...two large groups of people with radically different beliefs and cultures.*

raw materials /rɔː məˈtɪəriəlz/ PLURAL NOUN **Raw materials** are materials in their natural state before being processed or used in manufacturing. • *We import raw materials and energy and export mainly industrial products.*

restriction See Test 2 Listening Section 1

retailer /ˈriːteɪlə/ (retailers) NOUN A **retailer** is a person or business that sells goods to the public. • *Furniture and carpet retailers are among those reporting the sharpest annual decline in sales.*

spectre /ˈspektə/ (spectres) NOUN If you refer to the **spectre of** something unpleasant, you are referring to something that you are frightened might occur. • *Failure to arrive at a consensus over the issue raised the spectre of legal action.*

stock /stɒk/ NOUN A shop's **stock** is the total amount of goods which it has available to sell. • *When a nearby shop burned down, our stock was ruined by smoke.*

tailor /ˈteɪlə/ (tailors, tailoring, tailored) VERB If you **tailor** something such as a plan or system **to** someone's needs, you make it suitable for a particular person or purpose by changing the details of it. • *We can tailor the programme to the patient's needs.*

tariff /ˈtærɪf/ (tariffs) NOUN A **tariff** is a tax that a government collects on goods coming into a country. • *America wants to eliminate tariffs on items such as electronics.*

transformation /ˌtrænsfəˈmeɪʃən/ (transformations) NOUN A **transformation** is when something or someone changes completely and suddenly so that they are much better or more attractive. • *After 1959, the Spanish economy underwent a profound transformation.*

unprecedented /ʌnˈpresɪdəntɪd/ ADJECTIVE If you describe something as **unprecedented**, you are emphasising that it is very great in quality, amount or scale. • *The mission has been hailed as an unprecedented success.*

vast /vɑːst væst/ (vaster, vastest) ADJECTIVE Something that is **vast** is extremely large. • *Afrikaner farmers who own vast stretches of land*

visionary /ˈvɪʒənri/, US /-neri/ (visionaries) NOUN If you refer to someone as a **visionary**, you mean that they have strong, original ideas about how things might be different in the future, especially about how things might be improved. • *An entrepreneur is more than just a risk taker. He is a visionary.*

volatile /ˈvɒləˌtaɪl/, US /-təl/ ADJECTIVE A situation that is **volatile** is likely to change suddenly and unexpectedly. • *The international oil markets have been highly volatile since the early 1970s.*

GENERAL TRAINING TEST A: READING

Passage 1

betray /bɪˈtreɪ/ (betrays, betraying, betrayed) VERB If someone **betrays** their country or their friends, they give information to an enemy, putting their country's security or their friends' safety at risk. • *They offered me money if I would betray my associates.*

bohemian /boʊˈhiːmiən/ ADJECTIVE You can use **bohemian** to describe artistic people who live in an unconventional way. • ...*the bohemian lifestyle of the French capital.*

chopping board /ˈtʃɒpɪŋ ˌbɔːd/ (chopping boards) NOUN A **chopping board** is a wooden or plastic board that you chop meat and vegetables on. [BRIT] • *Vegetables were arranged in neat rows on the chopping board.*

corkscrew /ˈkɔːkˌskruː/ (corkscrews) NOUN A **corkscrew** is a device for pulling corks out of bottles. • *She fetched the corkscrew and two glasses.*

crockery /ˈkrɒkəri/ NOUN **Crockery** is the plates, cups, saucers and dishes that you use at meals. [mainly BRIT] • *We had no fridge, cooker, cutlery or crockery.*

dilemma /daɪˈlemə/, US /dɪl-/ (dilemmas) NOUN A **dilemma** is a difficult situation in which you have to choose between two or more alternatives. • *He was faced with the dilemma of whether or not to return to his country.*

duvet /ˈduːveɪ/, US /duːˈveɪ/ (duvets) NOUN A **duvet** is a large cover filled with feathers or similar material which you put over yourself in bed instead of a sheet and blankets. [BRIT] • *Use a thick duvet on top of your mattress for a comfortable night's sleep.*

hanger /ˈhæŋə/ (hangers) NOUN A **hanger** is a curved piece of wood, metal or plastic that you hang a piece of clothing on. • *He opened the cupboard to find a collection of suits and shirts on hangers.*

hygiene /ˈhaɪdʒiːn/ NOUN **Hygiene** is the practice of keeping yourself and your surroundings clean, especially in order to prevent illness or the spread of diseases. • *Be extra careful about personal hygiene.*

notorious /nəʊˈtɔːriəs/ ADJECTIVE To be **notorious** means to be well known for something bad. • ...*an area notorious for crime and violence.*

pillow /ˈpɪləʊ/ (pillows) NOUN A **pillow** is a rectangular cushion that you rest your head on when you are in bed. • *The sheets, blankets and pillows were gone from the bed.*

tumbler /ˈtʌmblə/ (tumblers) NOUN A **tumbler** is a drinking glass with straight sides. • *He took a tumbler from a cupboard.*

undercover /ˌʌndəˈkʌvə/ ADVERB If you are working **undercover**, your work involves secretly obtaining information for the government or the police. • *Swanson persuaded Hubley to work undercover to capture the killer.*

utensil /juːˈtensəl/ (utensils) NOUN **Utensils** are tools or objects that you use in order to help you to cook or to do other tasks in your home. • *The best carving utensil is a long, sharp, flexible knife.*

zany /ˈzeɪni/ (zanier, zaniest) ADJECTIVE **Zany** humour or a **zany** person is strange or eccentric in an amusing way. [INFORMAL] • ...*the zany humour of the Marx Brothers.*

Passage 2

chilly /ˈtʃɪli/ (chillier, chilliest) ADJECTIVE Something that is **chilly** is unpleasantly cold. • *It was a chilly afternoon.*

comply /kəmˈplaɪ/ (complies, complying, complied) VERB If someone or something **complies with** an order or set of rules, they do what is required or expected. • *Some beaches had failed to comply with environmental regulations.*

eject /ɪˈdʒekt/ (ejects, ejecting, ejected) VERB If you **eject** someone **from** a place or an organisation, you force them to leave. • *They went to the High Court in a bid to eject him from the business.*

engage See Test 1 Reading Passage 1

liable /ˈlaɪəbəl/ ADJECTIVE If you are **liable for** something such as a debt, you are legally responsible for it. • *The airline's insurer is liable for damages to the victims' families.*

negligent /ˈneɡlɪdʒənt/ ADJECTIVE If someone is **negligent**, they do not do something which they ought to do. • ...*claims against a negligent third party for personal injury.*

Passage 3

conduct /kənˈdʌkt/ (conducts, conducting, conducted) VERB When you **conduct** an activity or task, you organise it and do it. • *I decided to conduct an experiment.*

co-ordination /kəʊˌɔːdɪˈneɪʃən/ (coordination) NOUN **Co-ordination** is the ability to use the different parts of your body together efficiently. • ...*clumsiness and lack of co-ordination.*

frequency /ˈfriːkwənsi/ (frequencies) NOUN In physics, the **frequency** of a sound wave or a radio wave is the number of times it vibrates within a specified period of time. • *You can't hear waves of such a high frequency.*

frustrated /frʌˈstreɪtɪd/, US /ˈfrʌstreɪtɪd/ ADJECTIVE If you are **frustrated**, you are upset or angry because you are unable to do anything about your problems. • *She was frustrated that no one shared her sense of urgency.*

pin down /pɪn ˈdaʊn/ (pins down, pinning down, pinned down) PHRASAL VERB If you try to **pin** something **down**, you try to discover exactly what, where or when it is. • *It has taken until now to pin down its exact location.*

pioneer /ˌpaɪəˈnɪə/ (pioneers, pioneering, pioneered) VERB Someone who **pioneers** a new activity, invention or process is one of the first people to do it. • ...*Professor Alec Jeffreys, who invented and pioneered DNA tests.*

pulse rate /ˈpʌls ˌreɪt/ **(pulse rates)** NOUN Your **pulse rate** is the number of times that blood regularly beats through your body over a period of time, especially the number of movements that you can feel when you touch your wrist for one minute. • *Anxiety stimulates the blood supply, possibly leading to a high pulse rate and high blood pressure.*

replicate /ˈreplɪkeɪt/ **(replicates, replicating, replicated)** VERB If you **replicate** someone's experiment, work or research, you do it yourself in exactly the same way. [FORMAL] • *Tests elsewhere have not replicated the findings.*

respiration /ˌrespɪˈreɪʃən/ NOUN Your **respiration** is your breathing. • *His respiration grew fainter throughout the day.*

stimulate See Test 1 Reading Passage 1

GENERAL TRAINING TEST B: READING

Passage 1

donate /dəʊˈneɪt/ **(donates, donating, donated)** VERB If you **donate** something **to** a charity or other organisation, you give it to them. • *He frequently donates large sums to charity.*

fundraising /ˈfʌndˌreɪzɪŋ/ NOUN **Fundraising** is the act of raising money for a particular purpose, for example, for a charity. • *...a charity fundraising dinner.*

haggle /ˈhægəl/ **(haggles, haggling, haggled)** VERB If you **haggle**, you argue about something before reaching an agreement, especially about the cost of something that you are buying. • *Of course he'll still haggle over the price.*

Passage 2

approval /əˈpruːvəl/ NOUN **Approval** is a formal or official statement that something is acceptable. • *The testing and approval of new drugs will be speeded up.*

diversity See Test 1 Reading Passage 1

funding /ˈfʌndɪŋ/ NOUN **Funding** is money which a government or organisation provides for a particular purpose. • *Many colleges have seen their funding cut.*

incur /ɪnˈkɜː/ **(incurs, incurring, incurred)** VERB If you **incur** something unpleasant, it happens to you because of something you have done. [WRITTEN] • *The government had also incurred huge debts.*

integrated /ˈɪntɪˌɡreɪtɪd/ ADJECTIVE If several things are **integrated**, they become closely linked or form part of a whole idea or system. • *There is, he said, a lack of an integrated national transport policy.*

motivated See Test 1 Listening Section 1

policy /ˈpɒlɪsi/ **(policies)** NOUN A **policy** is a set of ideas or plans that is used as a basis for making decisions, especially in politics, economics or business. • *...the UN's policy-making body.*

priority /praɪˈɒrɪti/, US /-ˈɔːr-/ **(priorities)** NOUN If something is a **priority**, it is the most important thing you have to do or deal with, or must be done or dealt with before everything else you have to do. • *The government's priority is to build more power plants.*

submit /səbˈmɪt/ **(submits, submitting, submitted)** VERB If you **submit** a proposal, report or request **to** someone, you formally send it to them so that they can consider it or decide about it. • *Head teachers yesterday submitted a claim for a 9 per cent pay rise.*

Passage 3

compress /kəmˈpres/ **(compresses, compressing, compressed)** VERB When you **compress** something or when it **compresses**, it is pressed or squeezed so that it takes up less space. • *Poor posture, sitting or walking slouched over, compresses the body's organs.*

concrete /ˈkɒŋkriːt/ NOUN **Concrete** is a substance used for building which is made by mixing together cement, sand, small stones and water. • *The posts have to be set in concrete.*

deposit See Test 1 Listening Section 4

dissolve /dɪˈzɒlv/ **(dissolves, dissolving, dissolved)** VERB If a substance **dissolves** in liquid or if you **dissolve** it, it becomes mixed with the liquid and disappears. • *Pumping water into an underground salt bed dissolves the salt to make a brine.*

distinguishable /dɪˈstɪŋɡwɪʃəbəl/ ADJECTIVE If something is **distinguishable from** other things, it has a quality or feature which makes it possible for you to recognise it and see that it is different. • *This is vintage port, and it is distinguishable by its deep red colour.*

drill /drɪl/ **(drills, drilling, drilled)** VERB When you **drill into** something or **drill** a hole in something, you make a hole in it using a drill. • *A hole had been drilled through the concrete.*

fracture /ˈfræktʃə/ **(fractures, fracturing, fractured)** VERB If something **is fractured** or **fractures**, it gets a crack or break in it. • *One strut had fractured and been crudely repaired in several places.*

leak /liːk/ **(leaks)** NOUN A **leak** is a crack, hole or other gap that a substance such as a liquid or gas can pass through. • *...a leak in the radiator.*

lubricant /ˈluːbrɪkənt/ **(lubricants)** NOUN A **lubricant** is a substance which you put on the surfaces or parts of something, especially something mechanical, to make the parts move smoothly. • *...industrial lubricants.*

pit /pɪt/ (pits) NOUN A **pit** is a large hole that is dug in the ground. • *He lost his footing and began to slide into the pit.*

pocket /'pɒkɪt/ (pockets) NOUN A **pocket of** something is a small area where something is happening, or a small area which has a particular quality, and which is different from the other areas around it. • *Trapped in a pocket of air, they had only 40 minutes before the tide flooded the chamber.*

prolong /prə'lɒŋ/, US /-'lɔːŋ/ (prolongs, prolonging, prolonged) VERB To **prolong** something means to make it last longer. • *Mr Chesler said foreign military aid was prolonging the war.*

proposition /ˌprɒpə'zɪʃən/ (propositions) NOUN A **proposition** is an idea, offer or suggestion, usually concerning some work or business. • *These developments still offer the best investment proposition.*

reserve /rɪ'zɜːv/ (reserves) NOUN A **reserve** is a supply of something that is available for use when it is needed. • *The Persian Gulf has 65 per cent of the world's oil reserves.*

rock formation /rɒk fɔː'meɪʃən/ NOUN A **rock formation** is rock which has been formed in a particular place or with a particular shape or structure. • *...a vast rock formation shaped like a pillar.*

seal off /siːl 'ɒf/ (seals off, sealing off, sealed off) PHRASAL VERB If one object or area **is sealed off** from another, there is a physical barrier between them, so that nothing can pass between them. • *...the anti-personnel door that sealed off the chamber.*

shale /ʃeɪl/ NOUN **Shale** is smooth soft rock that breaks easily into thin layers. • *...the contentious process of extracting natural gas from shale.*

Audio script

Track 01

TEST 1   LISTENING SECTION 1

Customer: Good morning. I'd like to book a coach to London. I was hoping you had something available this Saturday afternoon.

Agent: Good morning, sir. Take a seat and I'll just check for you. Er, yes, we still have several free seats for Saturday. Where will you be leaving from? There are three pick-up points in town: Main Street, Centenary Square or the Central Bus Station.

Customer: From Centenary Square, please. That's easier for me to get to than the bus station.

Agent: And what time would you like to leave? There are coaches on the hour, every hour, from 12.00 through till 6.00 p.m.

Customer: Well, I'm meeting someone at the station in London and I need to be there for 4.30, so which one would you recommend?

Agent: Um, well, there's one leaving at 1.00. That arrives at Victoria Station at 4.10, if that's any good. Traffic is usually quite light at the weekend and the drivers tend to make good time, so I think you'd certainly be there for 4.30.

Customer: OK, that sounds just right. I think I'll take that. I can always phone ahead if I'm going to be late.

Agent: And when are you returning, sir?

Customer: Actually, I'm not sure when I'll be coming back, so I won't book a return ticket, just one way.

Agent: I can always book you an open return if you'd like. You can use this at any time within the next month as long as you contact us first to reserve a seat.

Customer: Well, there's a chance I might be getting a lift back, you see, so I'll just pay for one way. I don't want to buy a return if I don't need it.

Agent: OK, no problem. Are you travelling alone?

Customer: Just the one ticket, please. I'm going down to visit my daughter at university. My son's meeting me at the station, so it's a proper family reunion.

Agent: Very nice! OK. Well, I can book that for you if you like, sir. That'll be £23.50. Now, I just need to take down some details. Can I have your name, please?

Customer: Yes, it's Matthew Upton, that's U-P-T-O-N.

Agent: And your address?

Customer: 34 Allesley Road. Allesley, that's A-double L-E-S-L-E-Y.

Agent: And your telephone number?

Customer: 01732 558997.

Agent: And your email address. We'll use this to send confirmation of your travel details.

Customer: matt257@yahoo.co.uk.

Agent: OK, thanks.

Customer: Before I forget, I'll be taking a little luggage. Is there a set luggage allowance?

Agent: We offer a very good luggage allowance. You can take two suitcases as long as they're no more than 20 kilos each; that's 40 kilos in total, and one small item of hand luggage on the coach. Most people find that more than adequate. Any additional items carry an extra charge of £10 for each bag.

Customer: I certainly won't be taking that much, so I should be OK. I was worried I might be taking too much.

Agent: Would you like travel insurance included with your ticket? It's an additional £2.00.

Customer: No, I don't think so.

Agent: No problem, it's not compulsory. OK, how will you be paying?

Customer: Actually, I've been having trouble with my debit card today and I've left my cheque book at home, so I'd better pay in cash. You'll give me a receipt, won't you?

Agent: Certainly, and we'll send confirmation to your email address as well. So, that's £23.50, sir. If you just wait a minute, I'll print you off a receipt.

Track 02

TEST 1   LISTENING SECTION 2

Presenter: ... and welcome back to the programme. Today I'm talking with Mary Littlejohn from Meere Green Library. As you'll all know, we've sadly been without our local library for the past three months but the good news is that it's about to open again. Great news, Mary.

Mary: It certainly is, Jonathan. Despite the fact that money's in short supply, I think visitors will be pleasantly surprised at how different – and hopefully better – everything is. Fortunately, we didn't need to replace the roof as we'd originally feared. It just needed repairing, so we were left with more money than we expected. We've been able to replace all that old wooden shelving with a more modern style. The computers have been moved to a new designated IT room, and on the subject of technology, visitors can now order and return books and CDs on their own with our new automated system – so no more queuing to be served. Sadly, money ran out before we had the chance to decorate the meeting room but we're hoping to complete that next year. Oh, and the children's section now has some colourful new tables and chairs as well.

Presenter: That all sounds fantastic. So, are you having a big re-opening party?

Mary: Well, the doors open on 28th August and we'll be serving tea, coffee and sandwiches at 12.30. Then we get down to business in September. The local History Society will be meeting on the first Monday of each month at 7.30 as usual, and we'll be starting our Wednesday lunchtime Book Club at 1.00. Both of those events are in the meeting room. The Computer Club won't be running in September as we still need to complete work in the IT suite, but this will certainly be returning in October. And we're especially looking forward to welcoming a local writer, Sally Wainright, to a new event on 22nd September. This will be the first of a series of events we're calling 'Ask the Author'. Visitors will be able to hear authors read from their latest works, ask questions and even buy a copy of their book to take home.

Presenter: I might pop along to that one myself. Now, I understand you also have a request.

Mary: Yes, that's right. We're looking for anyone who has a few spare hours each week who would like to offer their services to the library. Our computer classes have become so popular over the past year that we're thinking about starting a second session and we'll need someone to run it. The current teacher will work with you, so you won't be left to sort things out on your own. We can promise the person a warm welcome and a class of very motivated people, many of whom are at quite a high level. We're also trying to do our bit to break down the generation gap and we've been inviting some of our older citizens in to talk to school groups about the past. The children range in age from seven to eleven – they're always accompanied by their teacher, by the way – but we haven't opened it up to teenagers yet. So, if you'd like to help out, please get in touch.

Presenter: And I also understand you've got good news for those who've been making use of the mobile library.

Mary: Yes. Because the library has been closed, we've been running a mobile library service and going out to people in the community. Well, feedback has been so positive about this, particularly amongst our elderly users, that we've decided to keep it going. Users can reserve books if the bus doesn't have anything that they feel like borrowing. There's a computer on board with access to the library database, so the librarian will be able to reserve one for you. Unfortunately, we don't stock newspapers or magazines on the bus as these tend to be for reference purposes only and can't be taken away. We're also pleased to be working with the local council, who've agreed to send someone from the community office on the bus. They'll be able to help you with any local issues you may have.

Presenter: Well, many thanks, Mary. I'm sure our listeners will be delighted to hear the service is fully up and running again.

Track 03

TEST 1   LISTENING SECTION 3

Tutor: OK, Fergus, so we've looked at your assignment, which was OK. Now, before you go, you know about the jobs fair that's coming up, don't you?

Fergus: Yes, it's the week after next, isn't it? The whole week, is that right?

Tutor: That's right. Monday through to Friday. I'd suggest making sure you get along there on Tuesday and Wednesday. Engineering companies tend to be more prominent then rather than on Monday or the end of the week.

Fergus:	Um, yes, I've got the programme for this year. And it looks like those days will be best for me. I'm only in my first year, so I'm not expecting too much from the day. But I've heard you can pick up some valuable ideas for career paths.
Tutor:	Well, you've still got a few years here, I know, but it's never too soon to make a good impression on potential employers. You've got the programme, so do some research. Have a look at company websites so you've got the basis for a good conversation with the people on the stands.
Fergus:	Yes, I was looking at one the other day. The boss was being interviewed about their staff development programme, and there are one or two other firms I'm also interested in.
Tutor:	Mm, that's good. You've made a start already. Remember to think about what you're going to ask people before you turn up. Not how much you're likely to earn, of course! You only discuss salaries at job interviews. No, questions about the skills you need for the job, the kind of personal qualities employers are looking for, that kind of thing.
Fergus:	Yes, I see what you mean. It's best to go prepared and make the most of the opportunities.
Tutor:	And I'm sure you don't need telling that it's a good idea to dress correctly for the event. You need to give off a professional air.
Fergus:	Well, I won't be buying anything special for the occasion, that's for sure. I've got a suit and tie at my parents' but I don't have time to collect it. I'll make an effort, though. A nice pair of trousers and a jacket, nothing too formal.
Tutor:	I'm sure you'll look the part. By the way, you'll often find companies have more than one representative, maybe someone from marketing handing out free gifts, someone who'll explain the interview process, an ex-student who now works for them, that kind of thing. Try and direct your questions towards the best person.
Fergus:	Yes, that's a good idea. I'd certainly be keen to talk to any ex-students that are around.
Tutor:	I'm sure you'll find the whole thing really useful. It's important to go to these events, and we always get great feedback from students who've attended. As long as you go with the right expectations. It's unlikely you'll come away with the promise of a job, of course. It's more about discovering what companies are looking for in potential employees.
Fergus:	Yes, plus they're a great opportunity to practise things like networking, meeting new people, talking about yourself and what you do, d'you know what I mean?
Tutor:	Definitely, yes. There'll be several high-profile companies in the engineering sector, and you'll have the chance to get to know some useful people. If they give you their card or contact information, make sure you keep it safe. It's a sign they like you and want you to keep in touch.

Track 04

TEST 1   LISTENING SECTION 4

Lecturer:	Many thanks for inviting me along today to talk to you about the results of some very interesting recent archaeological research.
	The saying 'you are what you eat' is often applied to present day dietary advice. Certainly, our bodies will show evidence of whether we eat healthily or live on fast food and take-aways. This can be particularly useful in archaeological research; through a careful analysis of the ancient bones of our ancestors, we can tell a great deal about their diet and the way they lived.
	I'd like to talk to you today about some research into the early settlers of some remote tropical islands in the Pacific. When these people travelled to these new lands 3,000 years ago, they had to bring along all the resources they needed for survival, including food, plants and animals from their original homes.
	One such group were the Lapita people, who were early settlers of Remote Oceania – several islands in the Pacific. When the Lapita set sail for the island Vanuatu, they brought with them domestic animals and crop plants. This allowed them to settle in an area where no humans had previously lived and that had limited natural resources. Archaeologists have been keen to discover to what extent these settlers and their domestic animals relied on the resources they'd brought with them compared to the native plants and animals they found on the island.
	In order to try and understand the diet and lives of the Lapita people, archaeologists analysed the chemical composition of the bones of 50 adults excavated from the Lapita cemetery on Efate Island, Vanuatu. Depending on what we eat, we consume varying amounts of carbon, nitrogen

and sulphur. As these chemical elements are ultimately deposited in our bones, the amounts, or ratios, of each one can provide a sort of 'dietary signature'. For instance, plants incorporate nitrogen into their tissues, and as animals eat plants and other animals, nitrogen builds up in their own system. The presence of different ratios of chemical elements may show whether a human or an animal ate plants, animals or both. Carbon and sulphur ratios offer another clue to diet. Carbon ratios, for example, differ between land and water organisms, as do sulphur ratios, the values of which are much higher in aquatic organisms compared to land-based organisms. As well as examining the settlers' bones, scientists carried out a comprehensive analysis of the chemical elements found in the settlers' likely food sources. This included modern and ancient plants and animals. They found that early Lapita inhabitants of Vanuatu may have searched for food rather than relying entirely on food they had grown themselves during the early stages of colonisation. In the longer term, they probably did grow and consume food from the resources they'd brought with them, but early on they appear to have relied as much on a mixture of fish, marine turtles and fruit bats, as well as their own domestic land animals.

The archaeologists believe that this analysis of diet may also provide clues to the culture of the settlers. For one thing, males had much higher nitrogen levels compared to females, which indicates greater access to meat. This difference in food consumption may support the hypothesis that Lapita societies were ranked in some way, or it may suggest dietary differences associated with the work people were involved in.

Additionally, the archaeologists analysed ancient pig and chicken bones and found that carbon levels in the settlers' domestic animals indicated that they were eating a diet mainly of plants. However, their nitrogen levels indicate that they may also have roamed freely, eating foods such as insects. This would have allowed the Lapita people to keep food resources that were in short supply for themselves, rather than feeding them to their domestic animals.

Track 05

TEST 1   SPEAKING PART 1

In this first part of the exam I'd like to ask you some general questions about yourself.
Have you got any hobbies?
What kind of hobbies did you have when you were younger?
Which hobbies are popular with young people in your country?
Let's talk about your leisure time. How do you usually spend your weekends?
What's your favourite day of the week?
What do you like to do to relax?

Track 06

TEST 1   SPEAKING PART 2

I'm going to give you a topic and I'd like you to talk about it for one or two minutes. Before you talk, you have one minute to think about what you are going to say. You can make some notes if you wish. Here is your topic.

Track 07

TEST 1   SPEAKING PART 3

We've been talking about the kind of things that get us excited in life. I'd like to discuss this subject with you with some more questions.
In general, what gets people excited in their daily lives?
In what ways can sport create thrilling moments for us?
Some people are thrill seekers. What is it that makes them crave excitement?
How would you advise someone to get more excitement into their life?
Do we get less excited about things as we get older?
It's often said that it's better to travel than to arrive. What does this mean to you?

Track 08

TEST 2   **LISTENING SECTION 1**

Katie:	Hi Jason. So what's the house like? I hope it's as good as the advert made out.
Jason:	It's OK. I think I've finally found something we'll both like at last.
Katie:	Brilliant! So what's it like?
Jason:	Well, it's within walking distance of uni, it's in a residential area, there aren't many students living there, but it's easy to get onto campus, and the city centre is only a bus ride away.
Katie:	OK, that's a good start. But what's it like inside? To be honest, when I saw the advert I didn't think it would be big enough for the three of us. The rent's not exactly cheap for the area. So come on ... Is it worth it?
Jason:	Well, it's got three bedrooms and a nice living room, so we'll all have our own space to work and somewhere to sit together. It's clean and there's no need to decorate. I'm sure your mum and dad would be happy with it, if that's anything to go by.
Katie:	OK. That sounds promising.
Jason:	And the landlady was really nice. She's not one of those people with a lot of properties. In fact, this is the only one she has, so she really looks after it. Her daughter was a student and stayed there last year, apparently.
Katie:	Good. The advert said there's no garage but I can park on the road outside. I checked and there are no parking restrictions along that road. I know there are some shops in the neighbourhood, so we'll be OK for food and basic things.
Jason:	Yes, that's right. It's a nice house. And the kitchen's fine. I suppose it's not exactly modern but it's clean and functional – all the things you need: washing machine, cooker ... There's no garden, which is a shame, so nowhere to sit in the summer. But there's Wi-Fi, so all in all I'm happy with it.
Katie:	Right, then. I think we've cracked it. I'd like to see it myself before we sign anything. I might pop along later to have a look. It's on Foxwell Road, isn't it? Let me just make a note of the address. That's F–O–X–W–E–L–L Road, is that right?
Jason:	Yes, that's right, number 94. I'll come along with you for another look. So, you know what the rent is, don't you? £430 a month. I know that's £50 a month more than we were expecting to pay but I think it's worth it.
Katie:	Mm, it sounds reasonable, especially if it's in a nice area. And we need to pay a deposit as well, don't we? According to the ad, that's one month rent in advance.
Jason:	Yes, that's right. That's normal when you rent, so I was expecting it. You'd better give the landlady a ring if we want to have look round. Why not give her a call and see if she's free later?
Katie:	OK, good idea. What's her number?
Jason:	It's a mobile number: 01764 445328.
Katie:	Right, I'll phone her now. Hopefully, she'll be free and we can go over there this evening.

Track 09

TEST 2   **LISTENING SECTION 2**

Presenter:	Today we're continuing our travellers' tales. On the line we have Amanda Toddington, who had quite a nasty experience in Australia last year. Isn't that right, Amanda?
Amanda:	Yes. My husband and I were on holiday and we were staying at a friend's house on the coast near Brisbane. It was towards the end of the holiday and I was about to go into the garden and enjoy my breakfast. I walked out into the kitchen, slid my left foot into my shoe and felt a tiny sting. It was pretty painless but I shook the shoe off my foot and saw this tiny spider running out as the shoe hit the wall. Anyway, not being an expert, I presumed the worst, that I'd been bitten by something that was going to kill me and I completely lost control. I don't think I've ever screamed so much in all my life. We'd been told beforehand to always check our shoes before putting them on as it's a common way to get bitten, so I suppose it was my own fault, really.
Presenter:	So, what was it that had bitten you?
Amanda:	Tony – that's our Australian friend – he immediately asked me if I knew what had bitten me, and I pointed to the corner of the room where I'd last seen the spider. He picked up a jar and found the creature in the corner, where the shoe had hit the floor. 'It's a redback,' he said, and he gently placed the jar over the spider. The funny thing was we'd been talking about some of the

creatures we needed to be careful of a few days previously, and as he said the name 'redback', the conversation came flooding back to me … In particular, the fact that the bite can be extremely painful. I've found out since that the redback is from the same family as the black widow spider, and it's the female that does the damage – which it turned out was what I'd been bitten by.

Presenter: You must have been absolutely petrified.

Amanda: You can say that again! I remember feeling quite confused. I wasn't in a great deal of pain to begin with, and yet I could see from our friends' faces that they were concerned. Tony explained that the venom, or poison, of the bite spreads quite slowly, so the pain doesn't feel too bad at first. Gwen – Tony's wife – brought an ice pack and Tony held it against the bite to make it less painful. Apparently, you're not supposed to put a bandage on the area as this can make it hurt even more. Tony tried to put my mind at rest by explaining that this was quite a common bite, that the hospital would have an anti-venom and that everything would be OK. But I was beginning to panic. We were flying back to the UK the next day and I really didn't know what to do.

Presenter: So what did you do?

Amanda: Well, Tony phoned the doctor, who told him to check my symptoms for the next hour or two. As time went on, the pain became very intense, from my foot right up to my knee. My husband was on the internet and was reading out the possible symptoms. I wasn't feeling sick and I hadn't yet developed a fever but I had a terrible headache and my foot was beginning to swell up. At this point, Tony decided to take me to the local hospital to be on the safe side. I really didn't want to go as I had visions of being kept in for days and all our plans being spoilt. But Tony and my husband insisted. When we got to the hospital, I was relieved to see how casual everyone was when Tony explained I'd been bitten by a redback spider. They told me to take a seat and got on with their work.

Presenter: And did you receive any treatment?

Amanda: By the time I got to see a doctor, the pain was very intense indeed and I was getting quite upset. The doctor decided to give me a dose of an anti-venom, which he assured me would eventually deal with the problem. Unfortunately, he also explained that it wouldn't have an immediate effect and the symptoms might last for several days. But the story has a happy ending. My husband managed to book us onto another plane one week later. And even better news was that the symptoms of the bite finally cleared up after about 24 hours. Within a couple of days, I was back to normal again. So thanks to the spider, we managed to extend our holiday by a week.

Track 10

TEST 2   LISTENING SECTION 3

Tutor: Anyway, as this is our first session, I'd just like to find out how you're settling in, how your Spanish course is going – basically, anything you feel you need to talk about.

Kevin: I'm OK, I suppose. I'm settling into my studies and I'm finding the course interesting. I've got a free day on Wednesday, which is good, and lectures and tutorials on the other four days. Yeah, I'm getting into the swing of things. I'm just missing home a little, that's all.

Tutor: OK. Well, if it makes you feel any better, I reckon half the students I speak with are a little homesick. It's only natural. Is this the first time you've lived away from home?

Kevin: Yes. I was thinking just this morning that I've never spent so long away from my friends and family before. I've been back home on one occasion since I started in September, but it's so expensive to get down to London by train that I can't go very often.

Tutor: Well, don't be too hard on yourself, Kevin. It's quite a lot to deal with at first, isn't it? Moving to a new city, being responsible for everything for the first time ever, shopping, cooking, etc. Then making new friends, and then there's your studies, of course, and getting organised. Are you living on campus or in town?

Kevin: On campus, in halls of residence. It's not as cheap as renting a room in a house but I thought it would be a good way of meeting new students. We're all in and out of the kitchen during the day, so it's not difficult to socialise. Like you say, I'm just a bit homesick.

Tutor: I'm sure that you'll find things get better over the next few weeks. Everything's new for you at the moment and a little overwhelming. But you'll get into a routine and start to feel more settled. What about Freshers' Week? Did you sign up for anything?

Kevin: Yes. I've joined a couple of groups. There's the Film Society, and a tutor recommended the Spanish Society, so I've signed up for that too. I've volunteered to help out on their International Food Day – making snacks, that kind of thing. And I'm looking forward to getting to know other members.

Tutor:	You said earlier you were finding your studies OK, so that's good as well. The main thing to remember is to try to be as organised as possible. You have so much more freedom to make your own decisions here, so it's important to structure your time to factor in time for studies. If you're on top of your work, you'll feel much more able to enjoy your free time.
Kevin:	Um, I was hoping you could help me with my essay writing. I seem to be spending ages writing and re-writing essays and, well, …
Tutor:	The best bet is for you to sign up to the university Writing Tutorial Service. They have people who are in place to support students specifically with these problems. To join, just fill in the application form and give them a sample of your work.
Kevin:	Brilliant! I didn't know anything about that. Can I give them one of my essays to look at?
Tutor:	They won't give you feedback on a complete essay, I'm afraid, as they may not be subject experts. It's really aimed at developing your academic writing skills. Ideally, you should write something between 1,000 to 1,500 words. If you find their page on the university website, they've got a list of general topics you can try.
Kevin:	So do I just turn up? Or do I need to make an appointment? I've got an essay deadline coming up soon, so I'd like to get help as soon as possible.
Tutor:	You'll need to arrange an appointment. The first step is to sign up for the service. Download the application form and essay title from the webpage. Don't forget to state when you're available for tutorials on the form. Email the essay and form to the team and they'll get back to you with an appointment time. It usually takes about one week from when they first receive your essay to arrange an appointment. You're usually given one tutorial a term but they may offer you further sessions if they think you need them.
Kevin:	OK, I'll do that. Thanks for your help.

Track 11

TEST 2   LISTENING SECTION 4

Lecturer:	Good morning, everyone. Today we're continuing our look at funding opportunities for small start-up businesses. The emergence of social media has given companies the ability to connect with fans and potential customers directly. On the back of the growth in social media, a model of raising finance has emerged known as crowdfunding. This revolutionary way of raising finance began with micro-lending in the nineties. More recently an equity-based model has emerged that allows people to invest directly in a new company. We're going to examine this in more detail later, but let's turn first to a third model, which I'll term a fan-based model.

With this model of crowdfunding, individuals are encouraged to give an amount of money to support the launch of a project or initiative without the promise of any financial return. Instead, there's a reward for donating. This contrasts with the micro-lending model, which would require a return on investment, and the equity-based scheme, which may offer shares. Crowdfunding portals or websites allow the business concerned to present the initiative along with the financial target required. There's a fixed time limit for fundraising and if the target amount is reached, all donations are paid to the company or individual. Whether it's an author planning to write a new book, an independent film company looking to make a new film, or a technology company with an idea for an app, the person or company needing funding would turn to its fan base for support. This is managed through one of the many crowdfunding online portals that have emerged. Of course, a fan or supporter of a particular initiative is likely to give money anyway. But donation-based crowdfunding will often make donating even more attractive by offering a rewards-based incentive scheme. Let's take a film company, for example, that needs funding for a new film. For a small set donation, the donor might be offered a free ticket to the premiere or a DVD of the film. A larger set donation might be rewarded by the chance to attend a launch event when the film goes live. Those people who make bigger donations could even be offered the chance to meet the cast of the film, whilst the highest level donation could see the person's name mentioned in the film credits.

For companies that already have a significant fan base, crowdfunding offers a fantastic opportunity to raise money quickly from a large number of people, each of whom donates just a small amount of money. Compare this to the time and effort that would be needed to sell your idea to investors or your bank manager, particularly in an age when raising finance can be difficult. The company may also have links with partner companies or organisations that run fundraising events. In this case, you can significantly increase participation by working with these organisations to promote your crowdfunding project. Another significant advantage is that you can reach out to your fan base for feedback on the project while it's being developed, thus making the final product more appealing. Crowdfunding enables you to raise awareness of the product at an early stage, thus increasing the potential for sales. With so many people behind you, it can also act as a great incentive to get the best possible product out on time and on budget.

However, there are disadvantages to bear in mind. The model can be described as 'all or nothing'. If you don't reach the monetary target required in the agreed time, all promises of donations are cancelled and no money is paid, leaving you back at square one. Should this happen, or still worse, you receive the funding but are unable to come up with the product, not only will your fans end up disappointed but the portal will record the fact that you failed to reach your target or that the initiative failed. Fulfilling all the pledges that you've made to people can also be very time-consuming. For example, remembering to send out copies of books or free cinema tickets can sometimes be forgotten in the excitement and frenzy of launching your product. People sometimes forget to factor in the cost of rewards when calculating profit margins, but these can be significant. And finally, if you have a small fan base, for example you're a new company or have a small social media footprint, raising awareness of your initiative will be challenging.

These drawbacks aside, donation-based crowdfunding is a wonderful opportunity for individuals or small start-ups to raise funds for that exciting new project whilst reaching out and connecting to the people who are most likely to support and promote your work for you.

Track 12
TEST 2   SPEAKING PART 1

In this first part of the exam I'd like to ask you some general questions about yourself.
What kind of books do you like to read?
Which do you prefer to read, e-books or traditional books?
Have you read any books written in English?
Let's talk about your friends. How often do you meet up with your friends?
Have you got a best friend?
Which qualities do you value most in your friends?

Track 13
TEST 2   SPEAKING PART 2

I'm going to give you a topic and I'd like you to talk about it for one or two minutes. Before you talk, you have one minute to think about what you are going to say. You can make some notes if you wish. Here is your topic.

Track 14
TEST 2   SPEAKING PART 3

We've been talking about the subject of letters and communication. I'd like to discuss this subject with you with some more questions.
Do you think letters will eventually be completely replaced by electronic mail?
Why might a handwritten letter feel more special to the receiver?
Are there some situations where we should still try to write letters with pen and paper?
Does email make our lives easier?
In which ways is the written word more powerful than the spoken word?
Do you think technological advances mean we have too much communication now?

Track 15
TEST 3   LISTENING SECTION 1

Receptionist: Hello, Mr Budley. Is that your treatment finished for today?
Patient: Yes. I've just had the X-ray for now. The dentist asked me to make another appointment to have one out and then to get my teeth cleaned.

Receptionist:	OK, let's have a look at what's available. I've got a couple of free slots next week on the 16th. That's the Wednesday. Monday and Tuesday are completely full, I'm afraid.
Patient:	Isn't there anything sooner than that? I'm in a lot of pain. Nothing this week?
Receptionist:	I'm afraid not. We're very busy this week. One of the dentists is away on holiday, so we're a little short-staffed. If someone cancels, I'll give you a call, but for the time being shall I book you in for the 16th? We have a free slot at 1.30 and another one at 3.30.
Patient:	OK, can you book me in at 3.30? Let me make a note of that. Oh, hang on. I can't make 3.30. I've got a meeting at 4.00 and I'll never get back in time. It'll have to be 1.30.
Receptionist:	Right, that's booked for you. Now, the extraction will be £90 and the X-ray is £20, so that's £110 altogether. How would you like to pay? Cash or cheque? I'm afraid we don't take cards.
Patient:	I'll pay by cheque, thanks. If it's OK, I'll pay for the X-ray now and the rest at my next appointment, just in case I have to cancel for any reason.
Receptionist:	That'll be fine. Just to let you know, we need at least 24 hours notice if you have to cancel, otherwise there's a £10 fee.
Patient:	So, the cheque. Who shall I make it payable to?
Receptionist:	Sinclair Dental Surgeons. That's S–I–N–C–L–A–I–R.
Patient:	While I'm here, I was wondering whether you had any information about dental insurance. I think my teeth are beginning to show signs of age and I might need a lot more treatment.
Receptionist:	Er, there's a company we work with ... Here's one of their leaflets. Their prices are very competitive and the cover they offer is similar to that of most other companies. They pay up to £650 a year for dental treatment and you can add your wife and children to the plan whenever you want with their family cover plan. This gives you a generous discount compared to individual plans.
Patient:	Thanks. It looks interesting.
Receptionist:	And they offer interest-free monthly payments too. Er, there's a telephone number you can call for more information.
Patient:	Thanks. I'll take it home and have a closer read. Will I be able to claim for the treatment I'm having now?
Receptionist:	Any treatment you have after your membership starts will be covered. So if you're quick, you might get the cost of work next week covered.
Patient:	Thanks again. Well, I'll see you next week then.

Track 16

TEST 3   LISTENING SECTION 2

Presenter:	Hi again. I'm joined today by Ben Knightly from the Media and Arts Centre. He's here to tell us about the launch of the city's arts festival. Hi Ben. This year has a particular focus, doesn't it?
Ben:	It does, yes. This year we want to encourage more people who would not normally describe themselves as being creative to get involved with some of our many events and workshops. Not simply turning up as spectators but to get involved themselves, to get their hands dirty as it were. There's such a wide offering this year that I'm sure we'll have something to suit all tastes.
Presenter:	You were telling me earlier how beneficial being creative can be for us.
Ben:	Absolutely. I recently attended a drawing workshop, and even if I do say so myself, came away with a very good sketch I'd done. But what was particularly surprising for me was my feeling of pride and joy when I looked at the sketch again and showed it to the family. It really took me back to the feelings I had as a youngster when I'd made something. I realised that even as an adult we can get just as much pleasure and happiness from creative activity. Actually, research has shown that the more we allow ourselves to be creative, the happier we feel; and the more positive our frame of mind, the more creative and the more curious we become about the world we live in.
Presenter:	Well, you've certainly persuaded me. So, what kind of events can we look forward to?
Ben:	We want to try and include as wide a range of people as possible this year, from people already involved in the creative arts through to elderly people who haven't been creative in years. So for example, we're inviting people in the creative industries who occasionally suffer from writer's block to join us on one of our creative walks. Walking has been proved to aid creative thinking and we're running a series of walks during the spring and summer around some of the many beauty spots in and around the city. Then there's our knitting programme. We're working with schools in the area to invite grandparents in to teach kids how to knit. It's a great opportunity to bridge the

generation gap and <u>rekindle</u> that interest in knitting you may have forgotten about. We also aim to inspire and support people without jobs through a series of free courses starting with creative writing workshops. These courses will give them an insight into the basic ingredients of a good short story and help participants get their ideas into shape. And for anyone out there who is looking for the chance to explore their creative side, come along to our printmaking workshops. You'll have the chance to study some fantastic prints by local artists, explore different print processes, and take home a print of your own to hang on a wall.

Presenter: Excellent. So how do we go about getting involved?

Ben: If anyone is interested in joining one of these sessions, it's important that you contact us first as places need to be booked beforehand. We ran similar sessions last year and demand was high. As I said previously, there's no charge for any of the workshops, and materials where appropriate will be provided on the day. You can get further information on our website and if you don't have access to the internet, call us on 514 2261. The booking office is open Monday to Friday from nine to five, but closes early on a Saturday at 12.30.

Presenter: Many thanks, Ben.

Track 17

TEST 3   LISTENING SECTION 3

Judy: Hi Graham. How you doing?

Graham: Hi Judy. I'm fine, thanks. And thanks for popping round. I was hoping I could pick your brains about transferring to another course.

Judy: Yes, I remember you saying you wanted to do something else. Are you planning on staying here, or are you looking to go to a different university?

Graham: No, I'm happy to stay here. I just feel I need to do something else. How did you go about your transfer? You did History of Art originally, didn't you?

Judy: That was the course I initially wanted to transfer to. I'd studied Art at college and wanted to continue but my parents <u>persuaded</u> me that English would be more useful, so I took their advice. But I really didn't enjoy it and tried to transfer to History of Art but the course was full. Anyway, I spoke with the course tutors and they told me about the Fine Art programme. They thought I had the talent to do it, so that was that.

Graham: I see. How did your parents take the news?

Judy: They were OK about it, really. They just want me to do what I enjoy, so everything's fine there. So, you're hoping to transfer as well, then?

Graham: Yes, I think I've given the German course a good try but I'm not really happy. Most of the other students on the course seem to have at least one German parent or they've spent a great deal of time in Germany, so their German is much better than mine. We get huge novels to read and I'm still struggling with the first chapter while they're already finished and writing their assignments. I thought about doing a combined degree, German with another course, as the workload would be less but in the end I feel a complete change would be best. One of my other subjects at school was History and I realise now I'm actually more interested in that. One of my housemates is doing History and it sounds like a great degree, so I've decided to focus on that.

Judy: Well, people do transfer, so it's not out of the ordinary. But won't you miss the opportunity to study abroad for a year? You spend Year 3 in Germany, don't you?

Graham: I know. Not only Germany, actually. You have a choice of Germany, Switzerland or Austria. That would be exciting, I know, but that's really the only thing I like about the course and I can always do some travelling after I've finished my studies. I still don't know what I want to do as far as a career is concerned, so I think it's best I study something I enjoy, first and foremost. Anyway, I thought I'd ask you about how you went about your transfer before taking it any further.

Judy: Well, the first thing you have to do is make sure you're clear in your own mind why you want to transfer. You'll need to persuade people that it's a good idea, so get your arguments clear. Then ... I'm sure you've already done this, but check what the entry requirements are for History and whether you've got the necessary qualifications. They might be more flexible now you're actually here but you need to show them you'd be able to keep up with your studies.

Graham: Well I've got History qualifications, so I'm hoping that won't be a problem. Who do I have to speak to?

Judy: Well, they always tell you to speak with your course tutor first in case there's a way of making the course you're on more appealing to you. But it sounds like you've definitely decided to get out, so

I'd go to the Careers Service next, just to make sure there aren't any restrictions on transferring. It shouldn't be a problem but it's best to check first. And then there's your funding. I'm no expert but I would imagine this won't be a problem; German's a four-year course and History is three, so you could just start from Year 1 next September. If the Careers Service think it's OK and there are no funding problems, go and speak to the Admissions Tutor in the History Department, just to see if they're happy with your qualifications – and if there are places.

Graham: OK. Well, I'm hoping it'll be OK. I'm planning to transfer at the beginning of next year rather than half-way through this year.

Judy: Yes, hopefully it'll be alright. If they accept you, it's pretty straightforward after that. It's not like you're going to another university. You just have to complete a form – I think it's called an internal transfer form. Your current Head of Department and the one for the course you're transferring to have to add their signature as well. And that's it.

Graham: Well, thanks for that, Judy. I'd better start making my case for transferring, I suppose.

Track 18

TEST 3   LISTENING SECTION 4

Lecturer: Today we're going to look at a fascinating condition that challenges the idea that we all see and experience the world around us in a similar way. For example, what do you see when I mention a day of the week or a month? What colour is the letter A? Or the number 10? If you often find yourself having more than the normal sense sensations, you too could have a condition known as synaesthesia.

Synaesthesia is a harmless but fascinating condition which is often described by psychologists as the joining of the senses. We normally experience our senses individually, so we *see* a colour or *hear* a word, whereas people with synaesthesia will find two or more senses being stimulated at the same time by a single stimulus. Some people will see or feel a *colour* when they hear a sound. Others will experience a taste or smell when another sense is stimulated. This happens automatically – the sensation can't be managed.

People often go through life unaware that they have the condition. A common response from individuals who learn for the first time that they have synaesthesia is one of surprise to discover that other people don't experience the same thing. It's a normal part of life for them and they will rarely describe the symptoms negatively.

To estimate the numbers of people with synaesthesia, one group of researchers sat people in front of a computer and showed them letters and numbers in black. Participants were asked to choose a colour for each character they saw. A small proportion of participants, namely those with synaesthesia, consistently described the same characters as having the same colours. On the basis of the results, researchers were able to predict that synaesthesia affects about one per cent of the population. This number has been confirmed in other research.

Synaesthesia takes many different forms but the most common is to see or feel a colour in relation to letters and numbers. It's commonplace for people to identify A with red, B with blue, and so on. Some people will actually see a colour, but in most cases it's a question of feeling or sensing the colour. However, it's just as commonplace to see days, months, letters and numbers spatially, that is in lines or circles, for example. People might say they see Monday up high, Tuesday just below Monday, Wednesday on the left, Thursday on the right, and so on. This doesn't mean that people with synaesthesia always agree on what they sense. Two synaesthetes will often argue over the colour of a letter, for example. But patterns emerge if a large enough sample of people are observed, providing clear evidence of this condition despite individual variations.

Colour and spatial synaesthesia are amongst the most common forms of the condition but they are by no means the only way people experience it. One of the more interesting combinations is word–taste synaesthesia. This occurs when words lead the person to experience tastes or certain taste sensations. So a person's name might have the flavour of a particular sweet, places might be associated with the taste of particular snacks. Taste needs to be seen in a wider context here. The sensation may be a feeling on the tip of the tongue or at the back of the throat and will differ from person to person.

Some researchers believe we are all born with the condition and that it's most prevalent in our early years but it then tends to become less noticeable as we enter childhood. It's a fascinating thought that as infants we experience the world around us through our senses in a different way than as adults. However, testing this hypothesis will be challenging, bearing in mind the difficulty of getting feedback from young infants!

Research also points to the fact that synaesthesia runs in families. In fact, as many as 40 per cent of synaesthetes, as they are called, know of someone in the family with a similar condition. This won't necessarily be a close family member and the condition may be traceable back to previous generations or to an extended family member such as a cousin or uncle.

There is evidence that synaesthetes are often creative and will often have artistic hobbies or interests. Researchers think this is not necessarily because synaesthesia makes them naturally more talented in this area but the fact that they have multiple sensory experiences generates an interest in, for example, art or music.

So that's synaesthesia. Apart from its intrinsic interest, for psychologists it's a fascinating indication that we may all experience the world around us in different ways. Once upon a time, these findings would have been regarded as highly subjective, lacking evidence and not of any scientific worth. However, we now have a much greater interest in how the brain helps us make sense of the world, and the study of synaesthesia is one way for us to discover more about this.

Track 19

TEST 3   SPEAKING PART 1

In this first part of the exam I'd like to ask you some general questions about yourself.
What kind of music do you like to listen to?
Do you ever go to concerts or music festivals?
Do you play any instruments yourself?
Let's talk about your English studies. Do you enjoy learning another language?
How long have you been learning English?
Are there any languages you would like to learn?

Track 20

TEST 3   SPEAKING PART 2

I'm going to give you a topic and I'd like you to talk about it for one or two minutes. Before you talk, you have one minute to think about what you are going to say. You can make some notes if you wish. Here is your topic.

Track 21

TEST 3   SPEAKING PART 3

We've been talking about clothes and fashion. I'd like to discuss this subject with you with some more questions.
Is it natural that young people should want to dress differently from their parents?
What pressures are there on young people to follow the latest fashion?
Are men less concerned about their appearance than women?
Is it true that the clothes we wear can make us feel more confident?
Is there an age at which people become less interested in keeping up with the latest fashion?
Does the fashion industry place undue pressure on young people?

Track 22

TEST 4   LISTENING SECTION 1

Police officer: Hello madam. I understand you witnessed the accident. Have you got a few minutes to tell me what you saw?

Woman: Yes, no problem. I don't have to be back at work for a while, so I'm pleased to help.

Police officer: Did you actually see what happened?

Woman: Yes. I was standing over there, near the bus stop. I was on my way to get something for lunch and just happened to be looking at a shop across the road. That's when I saw the red car come out from the junction over there.

Police officer: You don't happen to know what time it occurred, do you?

Woman: Well, I left work for my lunch break at one and it's only about ten minutes' walk away – the office, I mean – so it might have been about ten past one. Although I did pop into the shop for something, so it was probably closer to one fifteen.

Police officer: So it pulled out of Monks Road – that's the road over there – straight onto High Street?

Woman: That's right, yes.

Police officer: Did you get a view of who was in the car?

Woman: There were three of them. Two in the front, the driver, of course, someone in the passenger seat, and there was someone in the back. They were quite young. I doubt if they were much older than twenty. Anyway, they came speeding out of the side road over there and hit that lady's bicycle. The driver didn't bother to stop to find out if she was OK. He just drove off along the main road towards the town centre. Er, is the woman OK?

Police officer: She should be fine. She banged her head when she came off the bike, so we've called for an ambulance – they always like to check you out in case you have concussion. But no, she seems fine.

Woman: The bike doesn't look too good, though. I don't think she'll be using that again. I suppose she was very lucky, really. If they'd hit her instead of the front wheel, she could have been seriously injured. It looked like they were just in a hurry and didn't want to stop at the junction. I know the traffic lights aren't working there, so perhaps they thought they could just pull out.

Police officer: Could you give me a description of the car? Do you know the make and model?

Woman: Well, I'm not very good with cars, but I'm pretty sure it was the same model as my husband's car, a Ford Fiesta. It was red, like I said, and quite old, and the door on the driver's side was damaged. It looked like it had been in another accident some time ago.

Police officer: I don't suppose you had a chance to take down the registration number, did you?

Woman: I did, actually. Let me see ... Um, Y ... 4 ... 8 ... B ... Y ... W. Will that help you trace them?

Police officer: That's really helpful. It depends. It might be a stolen car, but at least we'll be able to trace the owner. If it wasn't stolen, then yes, we'll be able to find out the name of the driver. Now, would you mind giving me your contact details, just in case we need to get in touch about anything?

Woman: Of course.

Police officer: What's your name?

Woman: Mrs Stansfield. Rita Stansfield. That's S–T–A–N–S–F–I–E–L–D.

Police officer: And your address, Mrs Stansfield?

Woman: 19 Althorpe Road, Bradford. That's A–L–T–H–O–R–P–E.

Police officer: Have you got a telephone number we can get you on?

Woman: Yes, it's 0232 566788.

Police officer: And do you have a mobile number?

Woman: Yes ... 07834 889772.

Police officer: That's great, Mrs Stansfield. As I said, we may get in touch if we need any further information, but probably what you've told me is enough. Thanks for your time.

Woman: No problem. I'm glad to have been of help.

Track 23

TEST 4   LISTENING SECTION 2

Speaker: Many thanks for inviting me along to talk about saving energy in the home. This is a key issue for many people who now find themselves on tight budgets. So today I'd like to spend a few minutes going through some simple tips to help keep those energy bills to a minimum. I'll start with some easy, cheap ideas before talking about more major solutions later.

I think we're all aware of the importance of insulating our homes, and although I'd advise you to get it done, I appreciate it can sometimes be inconvenient to have building work carried out. And though they're growing in popularity, having solar panels installed on the roof isn't a cheap enough option for many of us to consider seriously. So what other steps can we take? Well, most people will make a point of turning the heating down when temperatures outside rise but they ignore other equally useful ways of saving energy when they're making dinner or doing their weekly laundry.

If you're living in a relatively new apartment or house, you're probably blessed with a cosy, draught-free living space. But for those of us in older properties, the chances are there are gaps all over the place where cold air is getting in. Walk around your home and place the back of your hand around window frames. Can you feel cold air coming in from outside? Get down on your knees at the doors. Is there a draught at floor level? Fix these draughts with some cheap draught excluders and savings in heating bills will begin straight away.

And are you using the latest energy-saving light bulbs? I'm not recommending you go around your entire property throwing out older ones and replacing them all immediately. But next time a bulb goes, make sure you buy an energy-efficient alternative. And what about heating? If you have radiators in every room, do you need them all switched on throughout the day? If they're on timers, set them efficiently. Then there's the laptop or your TV. Do you leave them switched on overnight or on standby? Don't waste money, turn them off. And that goes for lights as well. You'd be surprised how many people leave them on when they go out.

There are also guaranteed savings to be made in the kitchen. I'm always telling my husband not to overfill the kettle when he makes a cup of tea. Why boil more water than you actually need? When you consider how many times that kettle gets used every day, you'll appreciate just how much electricity can be saved by boiling what you need and no more. And the next time you're cooking pasta or potatoes, keep a lid on the pot. The water will boil much more quickly than if you leave it off. And if you've bought yourself a pressure cooker or steamer and it's sitting in the cupboard never being used, get it out – they're much more efficient than pots and pans.

Now, the refrigerator and freezer. If the fridge is next to the cooker, it's having to work harder to stay cold. But as I'm giving cheap, easy solutions here, a kitchen redesign might be out of the question. Still, there are other energy-saving steps you can take. Keep an eye on the temperature control. We often forget to turn it down in the colder winter months when a high setting is unnecessary. Also, remember to defrost the freezer frequently and try not to overfill it as this isn't the most efficient way of using it.

The washing machine is another potential money saver. A lot of people wash at 40°C but it's often OK to drop the temperature down to 30°C, with similar results. And remember to either wash full loads or select the half-load programme; again, a surprising number of people forget to do this. And is it really necessary to dry your clothes in a tumble drier? If you have a garden or a yard, hang them outside. Or if you're drying them inside, get yourself a cheap clothes rail rather than hanging things over radiators, which robs you of valuable heat.

Now let's turn to some of the help our local council is offering to householders to save energy …

Track 24

TEST 4   LISTENING SECTION 3

Oliver: Excuse me, is this seat taken?

Alice: No, by all means, have a seat. Are you here for the Open Day?

Oliver: Yes, I think I've just about finished now. I got here first thing this morning. What about you?

Alice: I got here a little while ago. I spent some time walking around the place first, just to get a feel for what it's like. I'm doing the organised events this afternoon. I thought I'd have a coffee before I get started. It's a lovely campus, isn't it?

Oliver: Yes, I love it. And the facilities are unbelievable. I've just been over to have a look at the sports centre. There's an Olympic size swimming pool, a gym, squash courts, everything really. All the high street banks are here, and the bookshop looks better than the one in town. There's supposed to be a big supermarket a few minutes' walk from the main entrance, so there's pretty much everything you need here.

Alice: Yes, I really like the look of it … Um, I wonder if you can help me. I think I need to register to let them know I've arrived, don't I?

Oliver: I'm not sure you *have* to. You can just pick up an information pack from the desk over there. And nobody asked my name or anything when I turned up for the events earlier. I just walked in. But you never know; they might check after to see if people have bothered to come to the Open Day, so I think it's best to register.

Alice: Thanks. I'll just finish my coffee and then I'll get started.

Oliver: So, is this your first Open Day?

Alice: No, it's my fourth. I've been to Sussex, Coventry and Birmingham so far. They've all got their good points. But being a bit older, I'm particularly keen on somewhere that has a few students my age on the course. Apart from that, they all seem to have great links to businesses, and there isn't much to choose between them as far as their facilities are concerned. How about you?

Oliver: I haven't been to any other Open Days yet but I'm hoping I end up here. I've just been to a presentation by the Head of Department. It sounds like a great place to do Maths – that's my subject. He was telling us about all the avenues open to Maths graduates and the kind of work you can end up doing. A lot of students go into finance, accountancy, banking, that kind of thing. I can't say that's ever appealed to me, though. My Maths teacher at college was telling me about the opportunities in the software industry, which I quite like the sound of.

Alice: Well, I hope you manage to get in. According to the letter they sent me, my department is doing something similar. There's a talk later this afternoon by the head. I can't miss that. There's also someone who'll be explaining about the year abroad. Apparently, you can spend your third year at one of their partner universities in Spain or Germany. I'm going to have to give that a miss, though, to catch my train. Oh, and there's also an exhibition area in the Physics Department with some of the things people are doing here. I'll try and catch that.

Oliver: There were a few second- and third-year students at the exhibition I went to. One of them gave me some great tips on finding work as well. I already knew about a couple of accountancy firms in the area that offer work experience. That's on a voluntary basis, though. But apparently the students helping here on the Open Day get paid, and the university advertises other jobs that come up now and again, so that's worth remembering. And a lot of the shops here are always looking for staff.

Alice: Mm, that's useful to know. I overheard someone saying there's a tour of some of the halls of residence in about half an hour, so I think I'll register and try to fit that in before I go to the talk. Are you thinking of living on campus?

Oliver: I've not made my mind up yet. I don't live far from here. My parents' place is just the other side of town. I could easily get the bus to campus, plus it would be a lot cheaper if I stayed at home. But it would be nice to get some independence as well, so I don't know. I'll have to see. But I didn't know about the tour. Would you mind if I tag along with you?

Alice: No, not at all. Let me just finish my coffee and I'll go and register.

Track 25

TEST 4   LISTENING SECTION 4

Lecturer: Today we're going to continue our investigation into the use of technology in plotting oceanographic migratory patterns and I'd like to focus specifically on creatures that we didn't even realise existed until very recently: pygmy blue whales. In particular, I'd like to talk about a high-tech method of tracking that researchers have used to find out more about these creatures.

Pygmy blue whales, which are one of several sub-species of blue whales, spend their lives in the vast expanses of the Indian and southern Pacific Oceans. They were first identified as a distinct subspecies in 1966. Before then they were probably confused with the Antarctic or 'true' blue whale, so it's only recently that researchers have started to learn about them and their migrations to and from their breeding and feeding grounds.

Scientists are interested in pygmy blue whales because although they are a very mobile subspecies, very little is known about their movements and their populations. Large-scale movements of whales are particularly hard to study, and what we do know about pygmy blue whales we've mainly learnt from examining whaling records. There are several populations of pygmy blue whales in the southern hemisphere and two main feeding grounds off southern and western Australia. Scientists were interested in testing their hypothesis that the pygmy blue whales feeding off western Australia migrate to Indonesia to breed.

To track the whales' movements, researchers made use of something called satellite telemetry. This refers to the use of a satellite-linked tag attached to a whale. When the antenna on the whale breaks the surface of the water, the tag communicates with a satellite system. The location of the whale can be determined when multiple satellites receive the tag's transmissions, much like how the navigation system works on a mobile phone. Researchers receive this location data in almost real time via the project website, which allows them to track the movement of the tagged whale from many miles away.

The use of these tags has enabled researchers to discover that pygmy blue whales do indeed travel northwards from the west coast of Australia in March and April, reaching the warmer breeding grounds of Indonesia in June. They remain there until September, at which time they then return to Australian waters.

In addition to identifying the migratory pattern of this particular population of pygmy whales, research has also shone new light on the whales' feeding patterns. It's usually assumed that whales go without food outside of the summer, when they leave their feeding grounds. But interestingly, the pygmy blue whales studied travel from productive feeding grounds off western Australia to productive areas in Indonesia and therefore probably still have the opportunity to feed whilst they're in their breeding grounds.

It is hoped that mapping the migratory movements of the pygmy whales will help conservation efforts for these endangered animals, and the study has enabled researchers to identify specific conservation issues. For example, the migratory routes of pygmy blue whales correspond closely with shipping routes. Consequently, researchers are keen to monitor whether this has any negative effects on the whales' behaviour. Baleen whales – these are whales that use filters to feed, not teeth – use sounds to communicate and to gain information about their environment. Clearly, as pygmy blue whale movements correspond to shipping routes, there is potential for the noise generated by ships to affect communication and hence social encounters and feeding.

Previously, researchers could only hypothesise that pygmy blue whales occupying western Australian waters travelled into Indonesian waters. Now that this hypothesis has been borne out by evidence, conservation efforts can be undertaken in a wider area than just Australian waters.

However, scientists aren't stopping here. A question mark still remains over the movements of the pygmy blue whales that utilise the feeding grounds further south, off the southern coast of Australia. Genetic evidence indicates that there is a mixing taking place between the population of whales in the feeding grounds of western Australia and the population further south. Researchers are keen to discover whether the pygmy whales from the southern feeding grounds follow a similar migration route to those from the west coast or whether they migrate to the subtropical region to the south of Australia. As a result, there are plans to tag the pygmy blue whales further south in order to find out whether they move through the same areas as the western population and are therefore exposed to the same risks.

Track 26

TEST 4   SPEAKING PART 1

In this first part of the exam I'd like to ask you some general questions about yourself.
Do you live in a busy area?
Do you have all the facilities you need close by?
Is it the kind of place where it's easy to get to know your neighbours?
Let's talk about your future plans. Do you have an idea of what you will be doing in ten years' time?
Do you like to make plans for the future?
Are there any big changes about to take place in your life?

Track 27

TEST 4   SPEAKING PART 2

I'm going to give you a topic and I'd like you to talk about it for one or two minutes. Before you talk, you have one minute to think about what you are going to say. You can make some notes if you wish. Here is your topic.

Track 28

TEST 4   SPEAKING PART 3

We've been talking about the impact that people can have on our lives. I'd like to discuss this subject with you with some more questions.
People often say teachers had the biggest impact on their outlook on life. Why might this be?
In which ways can other people inspire or motivate us?
Who tend to be positive role models, family members or media figures?
Which historical figures do you think have had the most positive influence on the generations that came after them?
Do people in the public eye have a responsibility to be good role models?
Which values would you like to pass on to your children?

Sample answer sheet: Listening

BRITISH COUNCIL

idp IELTS AUSTRALIA

UNIVERSITY of CAMBRIDGE ESOL Examinations

Centre number:

Pencil must be used to complete this sheet.

Please write your **full name** in CAPITAL letters on the line below:

| 0 1 2 3 4 5 6 7 8 9 |
| 0 1 2 3 4 5 6 7 8 9 |
| 0 1 2 3 4 5 6 7 8 9 |
| 0 1 2 3 4 5 6 7 8 9 |
| 0 1 2 3 4 5 6 7 8 9 |
| 0 1 2 3 4 5 6 7 8 9 |

Then write your six digit Candidate number in the boxes and shade the number in the grid on the right.

Test date (shade ONE box for the day, ONE box for the month and ONE box for the year):

Day: 01 02 03 04 05 06 07 08 09 10 11 12 13 14 15 16 17 18 19 20 21 22 23 24 25 26 27 28 29 30 31

Month: 01 02 03 04 05 06 07 08 09 10 11 12   Year (last 2 digits): 09 10 11 12 13 14 15 16 17 18

Listening	Listening	Listening	Marker use only		Listening	Listening	Listening	Marker use only
1			✓ 1 ✗	21				✓ 21 ✗
2			✓ 2 ✗	22				✓ 22 ✗
3			✓ 3 ✗	23				✓ 23 ✗
4			✓ 4 ✗	24				✓ 24 ✗
5			✓ 5 ✗	25				✓ 25 ✗
6			✓ 6 ✗	26				✓ 26 ✗
7			✓ 7 ✗	27				✓ 27 ✗
8			✓ 8 ✗	28				✓ 28 ✗
9			✓ 9 ✗	29				✓ 29 ✗
10			✓ 10 ✗	30				✓ 30 ✗
11			✓ 11 ✗	31				✓ 31 ✗
12			✓ 12 ✗	32				✓ 32 ✗
13			✓ 13 ✗	33				✓ 33 ✗
14			✓ 14 ✗	34				✓ 34 ✗
15			✓ 15 ✗	35				✓ 35 ✗
16			✓ 16 ✗	36				✓ 36 ✗
17			✓ 17 ✗	37				✓ 37 ✗
18			✓ 18 ✗	38				✓ 38 ✗
19			✓ 19 ✗	39				✓ 39 ✗
20			✓ 20 ✗	40				✓ 40 ✗

Marker 2 Initials		Marker 1 Initials		Band Score	Listening Total

IELTS Listening Answer Sheet reproduced with permission of Cambridge English Language Assessment ©UCLES 2015

Sample answer sheet: Reading

Reading   Reading   Reading   Reading   Reading   Reading

Module taken (shade one box):   Academic 🔲   General Training 🔲

	Marker use only			Marker use only
1		✓ 1 ✗	21	✓ 21 ✗
2		✓ 2 ✗	22	✓ 22 ✗
3		✓ 3 ✗	23	✓ 23 ✗
4		✓ 4 ✗	24	✓ 24 ✗
5		✓ 5 ✗	25	✓ 25 ✗
6		✓ 6 ✗	26	✓ 26 ✗
7		✓ 7 ✗	27	✓ 27 ✗
8		✓ 8 ✗	28	✓ 28 ✗
9		✓ 9 ✗	29	✓ 29 ✗
10		✓ 10 ✗	30	✓ 30 ✗
11		✓ 11 ✗	31	✓ 31 ✗
12		✓ 12 ✗	32	✓ 32 ✗
13		✓ 13 ✗	33	✓ 33 ✗
14		✓ 14 ✗	34	✓ 34 ✗
15		✓ 15 ✗	35	✓ 35 ✗
16		✓ 16 ✗	36	✓ 36 ✗
17		✓ 17 ✗	37	✓ 37 ✗
18		✓ 18 ✗	38	✓ 38 ✗
19		✓ 19 ✗	39	✓ 39 ✗
20		✓ 20 ✗	40	✓ 40 ✗

Marker 2 Initials	Marker 1 Initials	Band Score	Reading Total

Sample answer sheet: Writing

This is just one page of a longer booklet.

INTERNATIONAL ENGLISH LANGUAGE TESTING SYSTEM

●● BRITISH
●● COUNCIL   **idp** IELTS AUSTRALIA   UNIVERSITY *of* CAMBRIDGE
ESOL Examinations

WRITING ANSWER BOOKLET

Candidate Name: ....   Candidate Number: ....

Centre Number: ....   Date: ....

Module: ACADEMIC ☐   GENERAL TRAINING ☐   (Tick as appropriate)

TASK 1

_____

_____

_____

_____

_____

_____

_____

_____

_____

_____

EXAMINER'S USE ONLY

EXAMINER 2 NUMBER: ....

CANDIDATE NUMBER: ....   EXAMINER 1 NUMBER: ....

Listening and Reading answer key

TEST 1   Listening

Section 1 Questions 1–10

1 A	6 558997
2 A	7 257
3 B	8 C
4 Upton	9 B
5 Allesley Road	10 B

Section 2 Questions 11–20

11, 12 & 13 IN ANY	16 Ask the Author
ORDER	17 B
C	18 B
D	19 & 20 IN ANY ORDER
F	B
14 (local) history society	E
15 book club	

Section 3 Questions 21–30

21 Tuesday and	27 A
Wednesday	28, 29 & 30 IN ANY
22 career paths	ORDER
23 company websites	B
24 B	E
25 A	F
26 B	

Section 4 Questions 31–40

31 C	37 domestic (land)
32 A	animals
33 C	38 & 39 IN ANY ORDER
34 signature	B
35 land or water	C
36 ancient	40 C

TEST 1   Reading

Passage 1 Questions 1–14

1 v	8 A
2 vii	9 A
3 ix	10 bred
4 viii	11 agricultural crop
5 iv	12 man-made
6 C	13 cautious
7 C	14 long time

Passage 2 Questions 15–26

15 TRUE	17 NOT GIVEN
16 FALSE	18 TRUE

19 NOT GIVEN	23 A
20 C	24 B
21 A	25 A
22 B	26 C

Passage 3 Questions 27–40

27 B	34 macula
28 E	35 optic nerve
29 D	36 (industrialised) world
30 C	37 younger people
31 F	38 central vision
32 A	39 photoreceptor
33 cornea	40 injecting

TEST 2   Listening

Section 1 Questions 1–10

1 A	7 Foxwell Road
2 A	8 430
3 C	9 one / 1 month's
4, 5 & 6 IN ANY ORDER	10 445328
B	
C	
G	

Section 2 Questions 11–20

11 B	A
12 C	D
13 C	E
14 ice pack	19 days
15 bandage	20 a / one / 1 week
16, 17 & 18 IN ANY ORDER	

Section 3 Questions 21–30

21 C	26 application form
22 C	27 topics
23 B	28 available
24 B	29 a / one / 1 week
25 A	30 term

Section 4 Questions 31–40

31 B	36 feedback
32 C	37 awareness
33 time	38 cancelled
34 film credits	39 rewards
35 large number	40 new

TEST 2   Reading

Passage 1 Questions 1–13

1 TRUE	8 visible
2 NOT GIVEN	9 trees dying/dying trees
3 TRUE	10 root disease
4 FALSE	11 genetic tests
5 TRUE	12 underground
6 FALSE	13 normal
7 NOT GIVEN	

Passage 2 Questions 14–26

14 FALSE	21 B
15 FALSE	22 A
16 TRUE	23 C
17 TRUE	24 A
18 NOT GIVEN	25 B
19 TRUE	26 A
20 A	

Passage 3 Questions 27–40

27 C	34 C
28 C	35 A
29 A	36 C
30 B	37 B
31 C	38 A
32 B	39 B
33 C	40 C

TEST 3   Listening

Section 1 Questions 1–10

1 C	6 Sinclair
2 B	7 year
3 A	8 family
4 20	9 monthly / every month
5 24 / twenty-four	10 membership

Section 2 Questions 11–20

11 C	16 A
12 & 13 IN ANY ORDER	17 C
B	18 booked
E	19 materials
14 B	20 12.30 / twelve thirty
15 D	

Section 3 Questions 21–30

21 B	27 qualifications / entry
22 C	requirements
23 A	28 funding
24, 25 & 26 IN ANY ORDER	29 internal transfer
A	30 Head of Department
C	
F	

Section 4 Questions 31–40

31 B	36 A
32 A	37 A
33 B	38 A
34 C	39 C
35 B	40 B

TEST 3   Reading

Passage 1 Questions 1–12

1 vi	7 hypersensitive
2 iii	8 sensory cortex
3 ix	9 neurons
4 viii	10 trimester
5 ii	11 functions
6 stimuli	12 B

Passage 2 Questions 13–26

13 TRUE	20 B
14 TRUE	21 A
15 FALSE	22 A
16 FALSE	23 C
17 NOT GIVEN	24 C
18 FALSE	25 A
19 TRUE	26 B

Passage 3 Questions 27–40

27 86 / eighty-six billion	34 G
28 did not grow	35 F
29 shift (brain) functions	36 D
30 long-term (memories)	37 TRUE
31 spatial navigation	38 NOT GIVEN
32 more developed /	39 TRUE
better developed	40 FALSE
33 B	

TEST 4   Listening

Section 1 Questions 1–10

1 1.15 / one fifteen /	6 damaged
quarter past one	7 BYW
2 three / 3	8 Stansfield
3 bicycle / bike	9 Althorpe Road
4 town centre	10 889772
5 traffic lights	

Section 2 Questions 11–20

11 A	17 cooker
12 C	18 (colder) winter
13 older / old	(months)
14 standby	19 defrost
15 more water	20 thirty / 30
16 a lid on / lids on	

Section 3 Questions 21–30

21 B	26 C
22 A	27 B
23 A	28 A
24 C	29 A
25 C	30 C

Section 4 Questions 31–40

31 confused	36 September
32 population(s)	37 food / feeding
33 location	38 shipping
34 website	39 wider
35 west coast	40 subtropical

TEST 4 Reading

Passage 1 Questions 1–13

1 50	8 G
2 29.7 kilometres	9 A
3 20 to 30 / 20–30	10 E
4 36.5	11 C
5 54,000 kilometres	12 D
6 1,200	13 F
7 B	

Passage 2 Questions 14–26

14 A	20 high-tech
15 B	21 range of punishments
16 D	22 waste collection
17 D	23 fine
18 best (environmental) option	24 landfill sites
	25 burning
19 coherent strategy	26 D

Passage 3 Questions 27–40

27 E	34 C
28 A	35 B
29 D	36 A
30 B	37 C
31 F	38 C
32 C	39 B
33 C	40 A

GENERAL TRAINING TEST A
Reading

Section 1 Questions 1–14

1 FALSE	5 NOT GIVEN
2 TRUE	6 TRUE
3 NOT GIVEN	7 FALSE
4 TRUE	8 TRUE

9 D	12 A
10 H	13 E
11 F	14 C

Section 2 Questions 15–26

15 FALSE	22 coin toss
16 NOT GIVEN	23 rotation
17 TRUE	24 sweeping
18 NOT GIVEN	25 centre circle
19 FALSE	26 strategy
20 TRUE	
21 two / 2 hours	

Section 3 Questions 27–40

27 NOT GIVEN	34 TRUE
28 FALSE	35 A
29 NOT GIVEN	36 B
30 FALSE	37 A
31 FALSE	38 C
32 TRUE	39 B
33 TRUE	40 B

GENERAL TRAINING TEST B
Reading

Section 1 Questions 1–14

1 vii	8 NOT GIVEN
2 ii	9 TRUE
3 vi	10 NOT GIVEN
4 i	11 TRUE
5 ix	12 FALSE
6 iii	13 TRUE
7 FALSE	14 FALSE

Section 2 Questions 15–25

15 ii	21 NOT GIVEN
16 i	22 TRUE
17 viii	23 staff development form
18 iv	24 purchase request
19 iii	25 expense claim
20 FALSE	

Section 3 Questions 26–40

26 TRUE	34 pits
27 TRUE	35 one / 1 mile
28 NOT GIVEN	36 sealed
29 TRUE	37 earthquakes
30 TRUE	38 over-reliance
31 FALSE	39 (real) issue
32 FALSE	40 bridge
33 high pressure	

Writing: model answers

Test 1 Task 1

These two graphs offer an interesting comparison of the growth in wages in G7 nations between two different time periods.

The first graph looks at the years 2000–2007. For several countries, wages fluctuated year by year with small increases followed by equally small falls in income. For example, Italy saw slight increases of just below 0.5% in 2000 and 2001, followed by falls of a similar amount in 2002 and 2003, before picking up again in 2005, 2006 and 2007 with rises of around 2%, 1% and 0.5% respectively. In comparison, the UK, the USA and Canada witnessed wage growth in most years, with the UK hitting almost 5% in 2000. 2005 was the only year when a slight fall was registered. These figures contrast sharply with those shown in the graph for 2008–2012, particularly for the UK and the USA. During this period in the UK, four of the five years witnessed wage decreases of between 1.5% to over 2%. Similarly, wage increases in the USA were smaller, with two years showing slight falls.

The figures seem to reflect the changing economic conditions that emerged following the financial crisis of 2007 and suggest that this had a significant impact on wages, particularly in the UK and USA.

Test 1 Task 2

It goes without saying that the car has become an essential mode of transport both for commuting and leisure purposes. We have become dependent on it precisely because of its convenience. With no need to wait at cold bus stops or train stations, motorists can start their journey a few steps from their front door.

However, this convenience has had serious consequences. As people have become more affluent, the number of cars on the road has increased year on year. As a result, traffic congestion has led to huge sums of money being spent on road building programmes, which in turn has had an impact on the natural environment. Moreover, despite the introduction of cleaner, lead-free fuel and the promise of electric cars, air quality in major cities continues to suffer from air pollution caused by toxic fumes from cars. Add to this the injuries and deaths caused by road traffic accidents, and it quickly becomes apparent that policy-makers need to address these negative consequences.

There are steps governments could and should take to alleviate these problems. Firstly, public transport should be improved to such an extent that catching a bus or train becomes almost as convenient as travelling by car. Secondly, commuters should be encouraged to car-share with people who make the same journey. Fuel costs are a major drain on household incomes and motorists would hopefully appreciate the benefit of sharing these costs.

Clearly, measures like these will not lead to a major decline in the use of the car but they may help us reduce the number of car journeys made.

Test 2 Task 1

The graph shows the various reasons the business community made use of social media during 2012. Businesses are categorised in terms of size of the organisation, ranging from those with over 1,000 employees down to small companies with 10–49 workers.

Firstly, it would appear that the bigger a business is, the more likely it is to have a social media presence. Whether the purpose is to exchange information within the business itself, to recruit employees or to promote the organisation or its products, large businesses make a greater use of this technology. Secondly, while small businesses make use of social media for a wide range of reasons, they use them particularly for promotional purposes or to interact with customers. Over 30 per cent of small businesses will use them to promote their products or services, whereas nearly 70 per cent of larger companies will do the same.

The results perhaps indicate that while all companies make use of this technology for a variety of reasons, larger companies have greater resources available to maintain a social media presence or are more aware of the benefits it can bring.

Test 2 Task 2

We are currently living in an era when job opportunities are limited and there is a high level of competition for any vacancies that become available. As a result, employers can demand more in the way of skills and experience from applicants, which can lead to young people being turned down in favour of people with more experience.

There is certainly evidence in my own country to support this situation. When employment statistics are published, youth unemployment is always a particular concern, with numbers remaining stubbornly high. In addition, young people who are fortunate enough to find work are often in short-term jobs that offer little in the way of career progression. This situation is aggravated by the fact that older people who have been made redundant or who have only semi-retired are also actively seeking employment. Indeed, several major businesses, particularly those in the service sector, are keen to employ more mature people since they feel the older generation have better customer service skills as well as years of experience behind them.

Clearly, it is necessary that society should provide work for all who need it and it would be wrong to discriminate against someone on the basis of their age. However, I do feel that younger people need to be given the opportunity to develop the skills and experience they need to get them started in the field of work. For this reason, I believe companies should be encouraged not only to employ younger people but also to provide appropriate training and career progression so that youngsters do not find themselves trapped in dead-end jobs.

Test 3 Task 1

This line graph shows the amount of money in billions of pounds spent by people from the UK on visits abroad from 1993–2013.

By far and away the largest sum of money was spent on travel, which has experienced a huge growth and reflects the growing popularity of overseas holidays. In fact, between 1993 and 2008, expenditure on travel almost tripled from nine billion to almost 27 billion pounds. There was a sharp fall in 2009 to just over 21 billion, with figures stabilising over the next few years. However, there were signs of growth again in 2013 to 24 billion pounds.

Expenditure in other areas has been far more stable during this twenty-year period. Money spent on visiting friends or relatives rose gradually from around one billion pounds in 1993 to approximately five billion in 2013. The amount spent on business since 2000 has had a gradual increase with minor fluctuations, but since 2008 has remained fairly steady at around five billion pounds.

Test 3 Task 2

Huge efforts are made by national bodies to be selected as the host of a sporting event like the Olympics as this is seen by many as an opportunity for economic growth. However, opponents argue that this can be a waste of money that could be better spent on much needed public services.

Hosting a major sporting event certainly offers the chance for huge investment in the transport and general infrastructure that large-scale events require, and these can have real long-term benefits for the country concerned. In addition, there are significant opportunities for job creation, and in the case of the 2012 London Olympics, for example, a deprived area of the city was regenerated. It is also claimed that hosting an event can lead to increased tourism and can give the country the chance to show off its organisational and creative talent, which in turn may lead to future business and investment opportunities.

However, opponents argue that similar outcomes could be achieved for far less cost. They argue that investment in infrastructure should not depend on whether or not the country hosts a major event, and improvements should be carried out as and where needed. They also point to the huge costs of laying on security as well as the disruption such an event can cause to businesses. Moreover, opponents also question the benefits to tourism, arguing that people uninterested in the event can actually be put off from visiting the country.

In my opinion, hosting an event of this size does seem to be very popular with local people, and if long-term benefits can be gained, then it would appear to be a project worth participating in.

Test 4 Task 1

The infographics examine the numbers of people in employment in the UK in 2013, categorised by their proficiency in English.

Almost 28 million people between the ages of 16 to 64 are employed. Being in employment is heavily dependent upon a person's ability to use English proficiently. For example, nearly 72 per cent of native speakers will have jobs compared to 65 per cent of those who are proficient in English, and as low as 48 per cent for people who do not use English well. Men are far more likely to be employed than women, particularly amongst the non-proficient group, where twice as many men will be in paid work.

In terms of entering a professional occupation, people proficient in English have almost the same opportunities as native speakers, with around 17 per cent of these people featuring in this category. In contrast, the majority of non-proficient English speakers enter work defined as elementary, which is presumably unskilled work, but with a sizable minority (21 per cent) having a skilled trade.

Test 4 Task 2

Taxation is and always has been a major issue that divides people and is often what distinguishes one political party and ideology from another. Since few people enjoy having a significant chunk of their income stopped at source, the electorate will consequently often look favourably on politicians who promise to keep taxes low. Indeed, it is a brave political leader who proposes to raise taxes when standing for election.

In my view, taxation is essential if key services are to be provided but it is also something that needs to be more transparent. For example, there are certain services we all use to a greater or lesser extent. These services include everything from street cleaning to social services, from education to crime prevention. We all need the local council to remove our garbage and the police to keep our streets and ourselves safe. Taxation would appear to be the most effective way of paying for these services.

However, it is clearly a challenge to make people feel that the tax system is fair and works for the benefit of individuals and society in general. I feel that the answer lies in accountability. Technology is such today that we should be able to keep track of how governments and local councils are spending the money they raise from taxation and we should be able to hold them to account if money is not spent properly. This will not stop the debate over high or low taxation, but it will at least make what happens to the money we pay more transparent.

General Training Test A Task 1

Dear Sir or Madam,

I am writing in connection with some problems I have had regarding the leather sofa I recently ordered from your store.

To begin with, I was informed that the sofa would be delivered on Thursday between 9 and 12 a.m. However, the sofa did not arrive until 7.00 p.m., with the result that I had taken a day off work unnecessarily.

When the sofa finally arrived, I noticed several marks on the leather and pointed these out to the delivery man. He claimed these were just marks left by the packaging and would come out if I rubbed them with some cream for leather. However, I have not attempted to remove these marks as I feel this is not something I should be required to do with a new item of furniture.

I would therefore appreciate it if you would send someone to remove these blemishes as soon as possible. I also suggest you introduce a system to inform your customers as soon as possible when a delivery is likely to be delayed.

I look forward to hearing from you soon.

Yours faithfully,
Ana Boczek

General Training Test A Task 2

In my experience anti-vivisectionists tend to regard animals as having the same rights as human beings and believe they are entitled to be treated equally with ourselves. Not surprisingly, people with this view regard animal experimentation as cruel and exploitative. In addition to these moral arguments, anti-vivisectionists also point to evidence that such research is often worthless. As animals differ from us biologically, they argue that medical research based on animal experimentation will often have limited value.

On the other hand, many people accept such research as a necessary evil and argue that the benefits far outweigh the moral arguments against vivisection. Those holding this view no doubt feel that though animals have a right to be treated well, they do not have equal rights. They would argue that if we value human life more, we have to accept that medical research is dependent on using animals in this way. Without such practices, people would have exposure to drugs and chemicals that have not been tested beforehand.

This is a very emotive subject, but in my view, experimentation on animals, if carried out responsibly, is necessary for medical progress. As a society, if we are happy to eat meat, fish and poultry, it is difficult to argue against exploiting animals in other ways. With strict laws in place to control animal experimentation, I would hope animals are treated humanely and suffering is kept to an absolute minimum. I would also hope that researchers share their findings widely and avoid replicating experiments unnecessarily.

General Training Test B Task 1

Dear Marc,

I hope you and your family are well. It's fantastic news to hear you're going to be visiting the UK!

You didn't say where you were planning to stay but if you're anywhere near the Midlands, I'd recommend paying a visit to Birmingham. It's my hometown, of course, and also the UK's second city. We have lots of places of interest – museums, art galleries, a fantastic shopping centre and a brand-new central library that will take your breath away!

October and November can be a little chilly, so I'd advise you to bring something warm to wear. We also get a fair bit of rain at that time of year, so you might want to bear that in mind when packing your suitcase.

It would be great to meet up if you do decide to visit Birmingham. But even if you are thinking of another city, perhaps I could travel to meet you wherever you're staying. Let me know what you think.

Best wishes,
Geirant

General Training Test B Task 2

For many, the internet is their first port of call when they are looking for that special new pair of jeans or when they want to book the family holiday. The web not only offers the shopper a huge choice of products from numerous online stores but also the chance to take advantage of the best offers available at prices that will often be much cheaper than on the high street. Perhaps one of the biggest advantages is the opportunity to read feedback from other people who have already purchased the item you are interested in. Whether it is a book you are keen to read, an electrical item or a hotel you are thinking of booking, reviews are a very useful way of making sure you spend your money wisely.

However, shopping online means you forgo the personal touch you get at a high street shop. Moreover, it is not possible to physically handle products, which can be a big disadvantage. For example, shopping for food means you are unable to select the best fruit or vegetables available or check the sell-by or use-by dates. When buying clothes, you can't feel the quality of the material or try an item of clothing on before buying it. Finally, there is the issue of online security, which is a major concern for some people.

The high street offers us the chance to get out of the house and mingle with other people, and I think it would be a great loss if the internet led to the demise of this traditional way of shopping. However, the retail industry will need to adapt if the high street is to survive the revolution brought about by the internet.

Speaking: model answers

Test 1 Part 1

In this first part of the exam I'd like to ask you some general questions about yourself. Have you got any hobbies?
Not really, no. But there are things I'd like to do if I had more time, like painting and sketching. I enjoy doing that when I get the chance.

What kind of hobbies did you have when you were younger?
Well, like a lot of young people I used to collect things. I remember being very proud of my stamp collection – and I was obsessed with watching football for a while.

Which hobbies are popular with young people in your country?
To be honest, I don't think we really differ from young people anywhere. We like playing computer games – if you can call that a hobby. Lots of people do sport, but nothing in particular.

Let's talk about your leisure time. How do you usually spend your weekends?
My weekends always start on Friday night, when I go out with my friends to dance. That usually means I get up late on Saturday. I'll often go shopping in the afternoon, and Sundays are usually spent relaxing and getting ready for college the next day.

What's your favourite day of the week?
Friday, definitely. I have quite an easy day at college, so I'm often home by early afternoon, as I said before. I always let my hair down on a Friday night and it's something I look forward to all week.

What do you like to do to relax?
I like to read novels. I find I can get lost in a good story and forget about all the work I've got to do for college. And I always enjoy having my friends round to watch a film.

Test 1 Part 2

I'm going to give you a topic and I'd like you to talk about it for one or two minutes. Before you talk, you have one minute to think about what you are going to say. You can make some notes if you wish. Here is your topic.
...
OK, well, there are several moments I can think of. But I'd like to talk about something that happened recently as it's still fresh in my mind. This was about six months ago. It was a Saturday afternoon and I remember that it was raining heavily. That was important because it meant Dad didn't go to his football match. Instead, he came into the living room and announced that we should all get our coats on and go to the dog rescue centre to see if there was a dog we liked the look of. I couldn't believe my ears! My sister and I had been trying to persuade Mum and Dad to let us have a pet, and especially a dog, for months. I'd almost given up. It turned out they'd been secretly discussing this and had decided to give it a try. Anyway, you can imagine how exciting it was driving to the centre to pick our new pet. When we arrived, I couldn't believe how many dogs there were to choose from ... all different sizes and breeds ... But the strange thing was ... and what made it so special was that my sister and I both fell in love with one dog in particular. She was very small and was so pleased to see us. Her tail was wagging like mad, and we both fell for her instantly. To cut a long story short, we decided to get Bonnie – that's her name. We had to wait two weeks before we could bring her home, but now she's part of the family.

Test 1 Part 3

We've been talking about the kind of things that get us excited in life. I'd like to discuss this subject with you with some more questions. In general, what gets people excited in their daily lives?
I suppose it depends on your interests, really. I know my friends and I get excited about important sporting events – cup finals, that kind of thing. Getting together with your friends or family on special occasions can be exciting. Maybe it's an event that stands out from the daily routine that can get us excited.

In what ways can sport create thrilling moments for us?
Well, in football, for example, you never know how it's going to end until the whistle goes, so when your team scores near the end of the match and wins the game, it's probably one of the most thrilling moments I can think of, especially if it's an important game. And the fact that you're sharing the moment with others makes it special.

Some people are thrill seekers. What is it that makes them crave excitement?
I'm not a thrill seeker myself, so it's difficult to say. If you mean the kind of people that do extreme sports like bungee jumping or parachuting, I suppose it's about the adrenaline rush you get doing things like that. Perhaps if you've done something like that once, you become addicted to the feeling.

How would you advise someone to get more excitement into their life?
Hmm. That's a tricky question. As I said earlier, perhaps it's about doing different things. We all have our daily routines, and perhaps at the end of the day some people just like to relax and take it easy. Personally, I'd advise them to spend a Saturday at a football match. I'm sure that would work.

Do we get less excited about things as we get older?
Perhaps, yes. When you're young, everything is new or feels fresh – like birthdays, for example. Certainly, the older I get, the less excited I am about my birthday. Again, I think it's about doing something new and different. That can create excitement at any age.

It's often said that it's better to travel than to arrive. What does this mean to you?
Yes, we have a similar expression in my language. It means that the anticipation of something is often better than the thing itself. For example, people often get excited about a new gadget they're saving up for but as soon as they have it in their hands, it feels like a bit of an anti-climax.

Track 30

Test 2 Part 1

In this first part of the exam I'd like to ask you some general questions about yourself. What kind of books do you like to read?
To be honest, I'm not a big reader. I do read but usually when I've got plenty of time to relax. When I go on holiday, for example, then I tend to choose something that's popular at the time – something you find on the shelves in the shops.

Which do you prefer to read, e-books or traditional books?
I haven't bought myself an e-reader yet but I've used my mum's now and again. I can see why they're popular – my mum always says they're great for reading in bed as they're easier to hold.

Have you read any books written in English?
Well, in my English class we've been reading some English short stories, which I've really enjoyed. I think they're made simpler for non-native speakers but they're still interesting and a great way to learn new vocabulary.

Let's talk about your friends. How often do you meet up with your friends?
There are two different groups of people I like to call my friends, some of the people I study with here in the UK ... I see them all the time, of course, and some of us go out in the evening ... and my friends back home. When I'm there, we usually meet up at weekends.

Have you got a best friend?
Yes, I have. I've known Miguel for a long time. We went to primary school together and we've been good friends ever since. We live in the same street as well, so even though we've both left school, we still see each other regularly.

Which qualities do you value most in your friends?
I think the most important thing is that they're honest. If I ask them for advice or for their opinion, I like them to tell me the truth. It's also great if we share some interests so that we can do things together.

Test 2 Part 2

I'm going to give you a topic and I'd like you to talk about it for one or two minutes. Before you talk, you have one minute to think about what you are going to say. You can make some notes if you wish. Here is your topic.
...
I don't know if this is the most important letter I've ever received but it was the first one that entered my head, so I think it must be significant. It was the letter I received from the education authority to tell me which school I was going to go to when I was eleven years old. I'd finished junior school earlier that summer and I'd chosen the secondary school I wanted to go to. It was a good school and most of my friends had chosen the same place. Obviously, we all wanted to stay together but there was no guarantee that it would turn out that way. My family and I were on holiday when the letters were sent out, so most of my friends knew which school they were going to before I got home. I remember phoning one of them to find out if they'd heard anything and she told me that they'd all got into the same school. I had to wait until we got home to find out if I'd got in too. It was terrible. What made it even worse was that this all happened towards the beginning of the holiday, so I had to wait a whole week until we got back. I can still see the post box when we arrived home. It was full of letters and it took a while to find the one we were looking for. My mum opened it ... I was too nervous to do it myself ... and I remember the big smile she had on her face when she read it. I'd got into the same school as my friends! I was so happy! I think I left my parents to unpack while I went to see my friends to celebrate.

Test 2 Part 3

We've been talking about the subject of letters and communication. I'd like to discuss this subject with you with some more questions. Do you think letters will eventually be completely replaced by electronic mail?
I think they probably will, yes. The only letters I ever receive are official ones. I always communicate with my friends with email or texting. Some of my older relatives occasionally send letters but I don't think it'll be something my generation will do when we get older.

Why might a handwritten letter feel more special to the receiver?
Well, I suppose a handwritten letter is more personal. An email is just a collection of characters; there's nothing special about it. But each word in a letter is unique, if you know what I mean. The letter has been crafted by someone and that makes it of more value or gives it more meaning to the receiver.

Are there some situations where we should still try to write letters with pen and paper?
I think it depends. It's a thoughtful thing to do if you're thanking a relative for a present, for example, an elderly relative who might not use email. They'd appreciate a handwritten letter rather than something typed. But apart from that, I don't think so, really.

Does email make our lives easier?
For social purposes, perhaps yes, and because it's so immediate, it's a useful way to communicate at work. Although having said that, email can also be the cause of stress at work. People expect a reply to an email almost immediately, so if you have lots of emails in your inbox, it can be quite demanding.

In which ways is the written word more powerful than the spoken word?
I think it's because the written word is permanent. Once it's on paper, it kind of exists. The spoken word is gone as soon as it's uttered. Also, we have more time to think about what we write, so that can make it more powerful.

Do you think technological advances mean we have too much communication now?
Yes, I think that's absolutely true. There are so many ways to communicate with people – TV ... online newspapers or blogs ... email and text messaging ... I think we're bombarded with messages now, and a lot of us probably suffer from information overload.

Track 31

Test 3 Part 1

In this first part of the exam I'd like to ask you some general questions about yourself. What kind of music do you like to listen to?
I tend to listen to lots of different types of music, but my favourite is alternative music. I like to listen to tracks that you have to work hard to appreciate.

Do you ever go to concerts or music festivals?
I've been to a couple of festivals with my friends. They took place over two or three days and we all slept in a tent. It was really good – cooking food over a camp fire and staying up late listening to music.

Do you play any instruments yourself?
Unfortunately not. I've often thought about learning to play the guitar, and I've got friends who play who've offered to teach me, so I might take it up one day.

Let's talk about your English studies. Do you enjoy learning another language?
Yes, I do. It's hard work, though, and sometimes I feel like I'm not making progress. But it's also quite exciting when I listen to English or read an English newspaper and find myself understanding most of it.

How long have you been learning English?
For about two years. We started learning it at school long before that but I didn't really take it seriously. However, once I knew I wanted to go to university, I set myself a target of passing an advanced exam.

Are there any languages you would like to learn?
If I had the time and the ability, I'd like to learn a few languages. I was watching a man on the internet who could speak something like ten languages! I might try Chinese next – once I pass my English exams, of course.

Test 3 Part 2

I'm going to give you a topic and I'd like you to talk about it for one or two minutes. Before you talk, you have one minute to think about what you are going to say. You can make some notes if you wish. Here is your topic.
...
At first, I couldn't think of what to talk about as I'm not the type of person that gets excited about clothes. But then I realised I have a coat that I've been wearing for about two years. It's a three-quarter length coat ... it doesn't quite reach down to my knees. My girlfriend persuaded me to get it when I was going on a trip to Edinburgh and I needed something warm to wear. I'm quite tall, so short jackets don't really suit me and although I'd never owned a coat like this, she promised me I'd fall in love with it. It's really comfortable and keeps me warm on cold winter days. It's dark grey and what I really like about it is it goes with almost anything. If I'm dressed casually in jeans and trainers, it looks good, but if I ever need to dress in something smarter, I can wear it over a suit, for

example. Now, when do I tend to wear it ...? Well, I often put it on when I go shopping but you'll also see me in it if I visit friends or when I go out for the evening. I have to admit my girlfriend was right; whenever I go window shopping for clothes now, I'm always on the lookout for similar coats. Unfortunately, I don't think they're as fashionable as they were two years ago – you don't see quite so many of them around. Anyway, I suppose it's my favourite item of clothing because it was recommended by someone I care about and it's something I like now, but would never have chosen it myself.

Test 3 Part 3

We've been talking about clothes and fashion. I'd like to discuss this subject with you with some more questions. Is it natural that young people should want to dress differently from their parents?
Of course, yes. Part of being a teenager is rebelling against what you see as boring adulthood, and fashion is one way of doing that. The problem is that adults nowadays quickly adopt the style of clothes young people wear, so unless the fashion is outrageous, we all end up looking the same.

What pressures are there on young people to follow the latest fashion?
A lot of pressure! There's the effect of the media and the fashion industry itself. If you go into clothes shops, you can see that they all stock clothes that are in fashion. But more importantly, there's peer group pressure. People tend to fall into line with their friends and end up wearing the same style as their mates.

Are men less concerned about their appearance than women?
Er, possibly, yes ... But I think this is changing. My dad's generation and even more so my granddad's generation weren't that interested in what they wore. When I look at family photos, the men all seem to be wearing similar clothes, but men are much more fashion conscious now.

Is it true that the clothes we wear can make us feel more confident?
Definitely. I think we all have an outfit or an item of clothing we feel good in. It's not just that we think it makes us look good, but that we feel comfortable in it. I have clothes that I like to wear if I have an interview to go to, and other clothes that I'll wear if I'm going out somewhere special.

Is there an age at which people become less interested in keeping up with the latest fashion?
Well, as I said earlier, I think people today are generally more aware of what they look like than previous generations. They say sixty is the new forty, which means people of sixty have the same attitudes that people of forty had years ago. So perhaps it's only very elderly people who feel free to dress how they want.

Does the fashion industry place undue pressure on young people?
In some ways ... Certainly, girls suffer from this, and not just in terms of clothes. I think it's something that affects boys as well, but girls have the added pressure of having a good figure ... having perfect features ... That's why plastic surgery is so popular now. Women are under pressure to look just right.

Track 32

Test 4 Part 1

In this first part of the exam I'd like to ask you some general questions about yourself. Do you live in a busy area?
Yes, yes, I do. My apartment is only a few minutes from a shopping centre, so there are always lots of people walking past my apartment, and the traffic can sometimes be a problem, especially during rush hour.

Do you have all the facilities you need close by?
Yes, I do. As I've just mentioned, we have all the shops we need close by. Not big stores, but food shops, banks ... the kind of shops you need on a daily basis. There's also a great sports centre down the road.

Is it the kind of place where it's easy to get to know your neighbours?
Well, we know our neighbours on one side of our apartment. We always say hello and have a chat if we see each other ... But it's not a close-knit community, so people don't have much to do with each other in general.

Let's talk about your future plans. Do you have any idea of what you will be doing in ten years' time?
Not really. I'll be going to university this summer, so the next four years will be spent studying. After that, who knows? I haven't got any firm career plans yet.

Do you like to make plans for the future?
Definitely not. I think there's a time for that when you're older and you have more responsibility. I suppose I'm planning for my education, but apart from that I'd just like to see what happens.

Are there any big changes about to take place in your life?
Well, I'm sure university will be a big change for me. I'll be moving away from my parents, so I'll be independent for the first time. I'm really excited about that – and a little nervous.

Test 4 Part 2

I'm going to give you a topic and I'd like you to talk about it for one or two minutes. Before you talk, you have one minute to think about what you are going to say. You can make some notes if you wish. Here is your topic.
...

This is quite a difficult question as there isn't anyone who stands out as having had a big influence – apart from my parents, of course, who've been great. But there was a teacher at secondary school ... I have very fond memories of her and I think she influenced me positively. I lost interest in school when I was about thirteen. I don't know why but I became more interested in music and sport and didn't really pay attention to my studies. My teachers realised this was happening and a lot of them seemed to give up on me, but Mrs Thomas – she taught me Art – really made an effort to get me back on track. To start with, she always insisted I sit at the front of the class, right in front of her desk. You see, one of the things I'd started to do was to sit at the back of the class with my friends and spend the lesson talking and mucking about, so making me sit at the front put a stop to that. She was also really kind. I could see she was on my side, if you know what I mean. She wanted to see me achieve my potential and was prepared to spend time getting me to focus on my studies. I don't know if it was just down to Mrs Thomas, but I did get through that period OK in the end and I got down to work in time to pass my exams. Some of it was down to me but Mrs Thomas helped me make the right decisions.

Test 4 Part 3

We've been talking about the impact that people can have on our lives. I'd like to discuss this subject with you with some more questions. People often say teachers had the biggest impact on their outlook on life. Why might this be?
Well, in my experience the classroom was always somewhere you could discuss issues that you probably wouldn't be bothered to talk about at home, like politics ... the environment ... the subjects you're studying ... And the teacher usually has interesting things to say. So if you respect your teacher, you take them seriously and you're likely to take on board some of the things they say.

In which ways can other people inspire or motivate us?
Hmm. On the one hand, there are high profile people like sportsmen and women who can have a big impact on us, but sometimes it's local people. People you see doing good things in your community. I think they can motivate us even more because they're ordinary people just like us ... If they can serve the community, then so can I.

Who tend to be positive role models, family members or media figures?
I think members of the family are by far the most important, especially close family – your mum and dad most of all. If your parents set a good example in terms of how to behave ... how to treat other people, you can't help but learn these habits yourself. Media figures have an impact for sure but not as much as your family.

Which historical figures do you think have had the most positive influence on the generations that came after them?
I can't think of any individuals but it would be people who lived recently rather than centuries ago ... and they're probably going to be leaders of some kind, otherwise they wouldn't feature in our history books. People like Ghandi, perhaps, who was a great example of a man who believed in peaceful protest.

Do people in the public eye have a responsibility to be good role models?
We talked about this at school once and there were two different views. I think if you're in the media spotlight, especially if you have a young fan base, you need to act responsibly. But I know some people disagree and think celebrities are no different to anyone else really, that we all need to be good role models.

Which values would you like to pass on to your children?
I think it's important to be sensitive to other people's feelings, to be kind rather than cruel. Basically, to treat other people as you would like to be.

Acknowledgements

The publisher and authors wish to thank the following rights holders for the use of copyright material:

Test 1, Listening,
Section 4, Recording script / Audio script
Adapted text from: http://blogs.plos.org/
everyone/2014/03/14/3000-years-ago-ate/
Reproduced under the Creative Commons Attributive License
http://creativecommons.org/licenses/by/3.0/

Test 1, Writing,
Task 1
Figure 2a: Real wage growth in the G7 nations, from
2000 to 2007, from http://www.ons.gov.uk/ons/rel/elmr/
gdp-and-the-labour-market/q1-2014--may-gdp-update/
sty-g7-labour-market.html?WT.mc_id=7a1e7be5471
201e66315a4592d80dfce&WT.z_content=post&WT.z_
format=nugget&WT.z_taxonomy=lab
© Crown Copyright 2014
Source: Office for National Statistics and licensed under
the Open Government Licence v.1.0.

Test 1, Writing,
Task 1
Figure 2b: Real wage growth in the G7 nations, from
2008 to 2012, from http://www.ons.gov.uk/ons/rel/elmr/
gdp-and-the-labour-market/q1-2014--may-gdp-update/
sty-g7-labour-market.html?WT.mc_id=7a1e7be5471
201e66315a4592d80dfce&WT.z_content=post&WT.z_
format=nugget&WT.z_taxonomy=lab
© Crown Copyright 2014
Source: Office for National Statistics and licensed under
the Open Government Licence v.1.0.

Test 2, Writing,
Task 1
Adapted text from: http://www.ons.gov.uk/ons/rel/rdit2/
ict-activity-of-uk-businesses/2012/stb-ecom-2012.
html?format=print.
© Crown Copyright 2012
Source: Office for National Statistics and licensed under
the Open Government Licence v.1.0.

Test 2, Reading,
Passage 2
Extracts from 'Do You Speak American' from: http://www.
pbs.org/speak/education/curriculum/high/style/#
Reprinted by permission of MacNeil/Lehrer Productions.
All Rights Reserved

Test 3, Writing,
Task 1
Adapted text from: http://www.ons.gov.uk/ons/rel/ott/travel-
trends/2013/rpt-travel-trends--2013.html?format=print
© Crown Copyright
Source: Office for National Statistics and licensed under the
Open Government Licence v.1.0.

Test 3, Reading,
Passage 1
Adapted extract from 'Study reveals common bond of
children who hate to be hugged', by Melanie Reid from *The
Times Scotland*, 13 February 2010, reprinted by permission
of The Times/News Syndication

Test 4, Listening,
Section 4 Recording script / Audio script
Adapted text from: http://www.plosone.org/article/
info%3Adoi%2F10.1371%2Fjournal.pone.0093578
Double MC, Andrews-Goff V, Jenner KCS, Jenner M-N,
Laverick SM, et al. (2014) 'Migratory Movements of
Pygmy Blue Whales (Balaenoptera musculus brevicauda)
between Australia and Indonesia as Revealed by Satellite
Telemetry'. PLoS ONE 9(4): e93578. doi:10.1371/journal.
pone.0093578. Copyright: © 2014 Double et al. reproduced
under the Creative Commons Attributive License http://
creativecommons.org/licenses/by/3.0/

Test 4, Reading,
Passage 2
Extract from: http://www.wrap.org.uk.content/recycling-
continues-be-best-option reproduced by permission of
WRAP UK

Test 4, Reading,
Passage 3
'Hello 3D printing, goodbye China', by Michael Sheridan
from *The Sunday Times* 14 July 2013, reprinted by
permission of The Times/News Syndication

Test 4, Writing,
Task 1
Adapted text from 'Lower employment rates for those
non-proficient in English', from: http://www.ons.gov.uk/
ons/rel/census/2011-census-analysis/english-language-
proficiency-in-the-labour-market/sty-english-language-
proficiency.html

Test 4, Writing,
Task 1
Adapted text from 'Those who could not speak English well were most likely to work in elementary jobs', from: http://www.ons.gov.uk/ons/rel/census/2011-census-analysis/english-language-proficiency-in-the-labour-market/sty-english-language-proficiency.html
© Crown Copyright 2011
Source: Office for National Statistics and licensed under the Open Government Licence v.1.0.

General Training Test A, Reading,
Passage 3
Extract from 'The effect of background music on children with special educational needs and emotional behavioural difficulties – the Mozart Effect', PhD thesis by Dr Anne Savan, reproduced by permission of the author

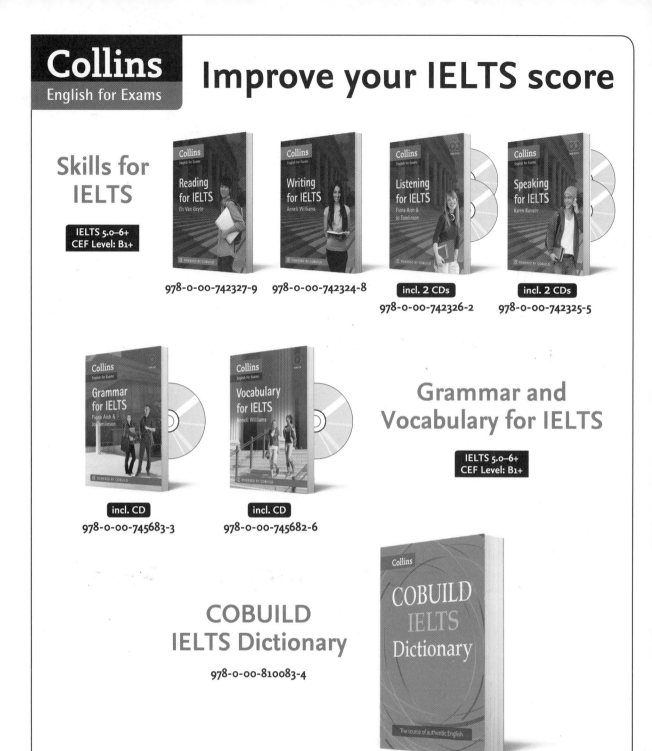